FROM NO TO NASDAQ

FROM NO
TO NASDAQ

GARETH SHERIDAN

Tara
PRESS

From No To NASDAQ
First Edition, 2025
Published by Tara Press
Dublin
www.TaraPress.net

© Gareth Sheridan 2025

Paperback Edition: ISBN 978-1-7392331-1-2
Electronic Edition: ISBN 978-1-7392331-2-9

This book is memoir. It reflects the author's present
recollections of experiences over time. Some names
and identifying details have been changed to protect
the privacy of individuals, some events have been
compressed, and some dialogue has been recreated.

All photos in the photographic section are the property
of the Sheridan family and used with their permission.

Cover design by Heidi Sheridan, Walker Lane Interiors

Printed in Ireland on responsibly sourced paper by
www.SprintBooks.ie

Dedicated to my Family

Table of Contents

Introduction

I'm Gareth Sheridan, and if you're holding this book in your hands, chances are you're on your own entrepreneurial journey or looking to make your mark in the world.

I wrote this book because I've lived the highs, the lows, and the long-haul reality of building something from scratch. As the founder of Nutriband, I started with a vision that most people didn't quite understand — a bold idea in health and wellness that pushed against the norm. What followed was years of learning through doing, failing forward, and staying committed to the mission even when the road looked uncertain or sometimes impossible

The key thing I hope you take away is the importance of people on your journey and it was no different for me. Without the support of my family and some close associates, advisors and mentors this story would never have become a reality. I am grateful for the chance to showcase the Nutriband journey (so far) in detail in this book.

Nobody's entrepreneurship path is the same but we can all learn from one another to make it as smooth as possible.

Use this book however suits you best: read it front to back, or dip into chapters when you need inspiration or clarity. But more than anything, take it as a companion – one that nudges you forward, reminds you of your potential, particularly when you think the journey feels lonely or difficult.

Through the highs and lows of any entrepreneurship journey remember that there really is no such thing as failure, it's just feedback. How you use that feedback to drive forward will ultimately define you.

Let's begin.

Gareth Sheridan
May 2025

FROM NO TO NASDAQ

1: Welcome to the Club

My Mum was picking up the messages for the weekend on a normal Wednesday afternoon when I phoned.

"What are you doing?"

"I'm in Dunnes Stores, just the usual. Why, is everything OK?"

"Everything is fine," I said, but I'm sure she heard the excitement in my voice. "We just got notice that we can ring the NASDAQ bell in New York! You are going to have to put the groceries back, I need you and Dad on a flight, you will have to leave for the airport in a few hours."

On Friday morning, December 3rd 2021 – just two days later – this 31 year-old from Terenure would be in the cordoned off VIP area in Times Square, with the NASDAQ countdown on the big screen, ringing the bell, opening trading on wall street and telling the world that my business, Nutriband, my college idea, was now a publicly traded company. It was hard to believe.

Mum was very cool. She just said, "Okay, I'll put the bread back so, and tell your dad and get on home and pack." And she did, and I picked them up in New York on the Thursday afternoon.

Then I told my brother, Aaron, that we were ringing the bell that morning and he said he would do his best to make it. When I added that we were going for a New York Steak after, he replied, 'I'll be there.' Unfortunately, he wasn't able to make it for the ceremony on such short notice, but he made sure to be there for the celebrations later that evening with his girlfriend Emily.

I also called my wife's parents Ned and Kathy and I told them what was happening. They were pretty excited too. They later admitted that they were unaware how big a NASDAQ listing was until their financial advisor told them about it.

"Come on," I said. "I'll take care of the flights and everything I just need you to get ready, you'll be flying out tonight on the red eye." In fairness to them, they said "no problem," packed their bags, and flew east that night with a couple of hours' notice too.

My wife Heidi was working on an interior design project in Florida that week, so she flew in as well that night, this was as big a day for her based on what she went through to get us there. We all got in pretty late, and the excitement was really building. Then my parents got in on the Thursday, and we all kind of took a big exhale – we were all there now, and I was actually ringing the NASDAQ bell in the morning. It was surreal.

The significance of the moment was, I suppose, that it legitimised everything I had been trying to do and accomplish. I imagine it is a bit like getting with that girl you were always after, you know, the one who only ever saw you as a friend!

For my company it was very important, because we'd been rejected by the NASDAQ twice. And now they were willing to put us on their banner, to have us open the day's trading for them, to trust us with that as well, when they wouldn't initially trust us with a listing.

"Ringing the bell" is a ceremonial thing more than anything, but it really brings everything home, brings it all to one place. We had actually been trading on the NASDAQ for two months at this stage, so it wasn't the first trading day, but it definitely solidified that we were home with the NASDAQ, that we were accepted, and that we were part of a very small niche of companies which had made it to that point.

Suddenly, we had credibility – that's what really changed. We went from a stock that trades on the Over the Counter (OTC) market – maybe three or four thousand shares a day – to listing on the NASDAQ, and all of a sudden, you're trading three or four hundred thousand shares a day. There's a liquidity change that's just astronomical.

I remember the first day we listed on the NASDAQ, I watched our stock like it was a movie for about eight hours. I just couldn't believe it. We'd traded a million shares, which at the time would have been a six-million-dollar spend, and I'm thinking, 'people I don't even know right across the country are buying and selling shares in the company that a few years ago was just an idea – a business school thesis.' It was hard to believe, watching it trade.

On the OTC market there are a lot of games played. You can run up to $40 one day, and you could be down to $2 the next day. And that's all trades of maybe only 500 shares – yet it can move it like that.

On the NASDAQ, it's a different level, it opens doors. All of a sudden, we were getting phone calls from the type of companies and investors who wouldn't answer the phone to us only months before. It was a complete 180-degree change, credibility not only for the company, but for me as a founder, as a CEO.

It all happened overnight, it didn't build to that point. On September 30, we were an OTC company and couldn't really make strides, and on October 1, we were a NASADAQ company and the phones were ringing off the hook.

It was mental. We had all these companies that wanted to work with us. Media people were calling, we had investor relations companies that wanted to work with us, and we had banks that wanted to do our next fund raise. The only way to describe it was a complete dive right into the deep end.

I loved it personally. It was a 'finally' moment for me ... where finally everybody else saw what we had been seeing. Finally the partners that we wanted to work with could see that we were legitimate. I think that was the other thing, it gave us a legitimacy.

Over The Counter companies can have a bad reputation, so we had always acted properly, like we were already a NASDAQ company. Our filings were always on time, our press releases were always right, we never pushed boundaries, we didn't try and pump the stock.

As it turns out, you can act like that all you want, but without getting that rubber stamp of approval – almost like, welcome to the big club – you are not really getting anywhere. But now we had made it.

Everyone has heard of kitchen table businesses, and the dreamers who think that world domination beckons. And yes, I am happy to admit I am one of them. I don't know why I first started thinking about the NASDAQ, but it has always been there for me. It is basically the Mecca for any aspiring business student with an idea. I genuinely can't remember ever not believing in what I was trying to do, and partners along the way like Serguei Melnik can be credited with driving that belief. I knew there were things I was going to have to weather, and that some challenges were going to be bigger than others, and some things would cause delays.

But I always saw myself ringing the bell. I didn't know when – but I could always see it. It was like I had the frame, and I just needed to put the picture inside. Then as I got further along, I didn't have a choice. Once you've taken people's money, you had better make it work. You do what you need to do to get it done. You can't possibly start feeling sorry for yourself or quitting because times are tough.

Tough times make for tough people and I wouldn't change a single thing in the journey, because if it had gone smoothly, I don't necessarily know if I would like the person I am today. I don't know if I would appreciate what we have, and I don't think I'd be as hard a worker as I am now.

No matter what the share price is trading at, $7.30 today or $730 tomorrow, I'm always going to remember picking pennies from between the front seats of the car and put a value on that. I don't classify the successful part of it monetarily. The main part that drives me –

the thing that keeps me going – is the impact that our products could have on thousands of people directly and indirectly.

Nutriband is a patient-focused pharmaceutical company with the aim of making pain medications accessible to those in need, and making them inaccessible to those who could abuse them. The ultimate goal is to revolutionize the safety profile of easily abused medications, primarily to give much greater access to the pain community which has been overlooked and undertreated for many years now mainly down to the negative stigma associated with pain meds such as opioids.

And then equally as important is the prevention of accidental exposure. This is a data point that we've developed a focus on while working with the Poison Control Center, where children are accidentally getting their hands on discarded pain patches, putting them in their mouths with serious and often fatal outcomes. This is something we're trying to tackle, and unfortunately today, has resulted in infant deaths and hospitalisations every year. We're trying to clean up a segment of the industry, the pain space, and reduce the stigma associated with pain medications, because pain patients are just as important as any other patient.

When we started, we focused on supplement and nutraceutical types of products, always with the goal to grow into the pharmaceutical space. Now that we've achieved that goal, and if our plans come together with our technology, AVERSA, I firmly believe that we will be one of the largest pain management pharmaceutical companies in the world and we will set the standard for safe and responsible pain management.

We're not just talking about people with serious medical conditions, or people suffering from severe pain. What about the families left behind because of the suicides among people who just can't bear the pain anymore, who cannot access adequate care? What about the patients who cannot access opioids to manage chronic pain who are forced into buying illegal drugs off the street and who accidently overdose as a result? I think it is only recently that we've started to really see the impact of what we are doing.

The lightbulb moment for me, the moment I became interested in medical patch technology, was when I spotted a patch on my dad's arm one day, many years ago. It was around the beginning of fourth year in the Dublin Institute of Technology – now TUD – when we were challenged to start thinking of our thesis idea. I knew I wanted to be my own boss and do my own thing, but I just didn't know what it was yet.

I was very into health and wellness and fitness at the time and was just thinking about it one day at home when my dad came in wearing a nitroglycerin patch. It is prescribed to prevent angina as well as lower blood pressure. It works by opening up the arteries and allowing the blood to flow a bit easier. I just thought that the technology was really interesting, and began reading up on it, thinking how people might be able get their vitamins for example, or even other medications in that way.

Originally I was interested in the diabetes space for my idea. But later, the opioid pain management issue began really hitting the news: the over-prescribing scandal, the abuses and the deaths from Oxycontin. By the time I was up and running, it made sense for us to focus on an area that everybody else was running away from. I thought – let me jump on this. Let's be the guys that fix this for people instead of running away from it. You had all those multi-billion dollar companies like Mallinckrodt and Endo and Purdue being sued for hundreds of millions of dollars because of their association with the bad end of opiates and opioids.

I remember thinking, who is going to sue me? I don't have anything. Why don't we just try and be the good guys here, try to fix a problem. I knew there was a huge pain community worldwide that everyone was running away from, real people who could not get their prescriptions anymore, and who were seriously suffering.

The reality is that prescription rates on opioids have gone down by anything up to 75% since 2016, based on the drop in the market size. But pain patients have actually increased in the same period. So the disconnect is huge. You have people who are suffering from uncontrollable pain who can no longer get a prescription for the only thing that will work for them – opioid and opiate medications. To manage that pain, they are now trying to buy opiates illegally, which is feeding criminality.

When I heard of the big companies running away from it once they could still make money from their shareholders, I was disgusted. As a Pharma company, you have a duty to make sure that people are receiving their treatments.

You can still make money in your business while being people-focused, but traditional healthcare is far too profit-focused. That's where there's a huge flaw in the system, in my opinion, just from what I've experienced in my relatively short time in the space.

Where there is a value on people's lives, companies will find a way to adjust it to their advantage. There is a case study we reference in many of our discussions. Back in the 70s, a major car manufacturer had an issue with the breaks on one of their models which they estimated would affect something like 0.3% of the cars they built. They calculated that the cost of a recall would be more than the cost of the compensation they'd need to pay out to the families of victims who died or were injured in crashes. So they just let it go. And you see that sort of thing in Pharma all the time, that cold actuarial look at the numbers – without thinking of individual people's lives.

One thing I really like about what we will do is that we will make other Pharma companies look bad. We want to be disruptive; we want to be the new name, we want to be a people-focused Pharma company, which historically doesn't exist in my opinion.

We have been told that when we get FDA approval, we could charge a 500 percent premium because we're adding this new technology. But we are actually going to come in at a 20 percent premium, which is something that's typically never seen.

How that works is that the higher the premium, the higher the reduction in coverage, which means the fewer the patients that can access the products, which means we would not be a patient-focused Pharma company. We know we will be a billion-dollar company anyway, and at the same time still be able to make sure everybody that needs the medications will get them. What many don't understand is that in a position like ours, charging a smaller premium and cornering or taking over the market will be far more valuable to us as a company and to our shareholders financially than overcharging for the product and taking a market share. If played correctly, we may become the only company in our space doing what we do. The lesson? You can be a successful company and still do good. And if we build a $100,000 investment into a billion-dollar company, I think that will prove our theory.

With our strategy, we can still employ plenty of people, we can still re-invest, we can still have new products, we can still give our shareholders a great return, and we can still make a difference at that size. I wouldn't be able to sleep at night if we were a multi-billion-dollar company that had succeeded at the expense of people not being able to access our products, but becoming a market leader and doing so at the expense of our competitors and not the patient is a great feeling. To look at it in another way, it gives us the opportunity to maintain coverage for patients but also look at cornering a market rather than taking a smaller share because of a reduction in coverage. Technically and fundamentally, our reasonable pricing offers us an opportunity to make a better financial return for our shareholders which many companies in our space tend to overlook and it is done so at the expense of our competition not the patient.

At every presentation I make, somebody comes up to me afterwards who has a family member who is suffering from chronic pain, and who can't access the relief they need. I've heard several stories of people who took their own lives because they could not bear the pain. If our product had been on the market, many of those people might still be here. Yes, there are huge addiction issues, but rather than just annihilate an effective pain management treatment, why not fix the way it is prescribed and delivered? And that's the solution we worked on. Because the pain population worldwide is equally as important as the addiction population, and they've been completely overlooked for almost ten years now. Our abuse deterrent technology, AVERSA, will make sure that the opportunity for abuse is severely limited, while delivering relief to many, many people.

Now, a few years on with my company, we are close to having a major impact on this. And I think that helps so much with drive and direction. It was never an option to pack it all in and go home. Along the way, as some people may know, we have had serious challenges, which I'll talk more about later. At one point, the Securities Exchange Commission (SEC) took a case against us. Even if that SEC case had succeeded, if a separate lawsuit had gone against us, even if I had got the lifetime director ban, I would still have had some role in the company – maybe just an advisor – but I would have kept wanting things to work.

The SEC were never going to get hold of my shares, I would always have had that. And maybe that is the thing I like best, taking on the seemingly impossible, and getting past it. When everything is thrown at you, when everyone is saying it won't work – that's a position I like being in. So as negative as the story sounds in parts, and as awful as the repeated challenges sound, it wasn't a playing field that I was uncomfortable in, and of course you really appreciate your wins then, as they happen.

I learned from very early on that challenges are good for you and are part of the learning process. A scenario that comes to mind goes back to one cold day, as a teen back in Dublin. I was raging with my dad on this particular day, typical teenager, unaware of the massive impact this lesson would have on me as I grew older. It was my first experience of painting houses, and I was freezing. I was about 13 or 14, and like every other kid in the country, I wanted the new Nokia phone, the 3310. Everyone was getting it, and everyone was playing Snake on it, and I didn't have one.

So I asked my dad for the €50 or whatever it was to buy the phone. And Dad said, "Of course you can have the phone, all you have to do is come to work with me tomorrow and you can earn the money to buy it." I think he purposely picked a freezing cold day. We were working outside a house in Crumlin, I was painting the windows, trying to learn what to do, but I was slow. After a while I turned to him and said, "You do this every day?" And he said, "Of course I do".

And maybe that's all you need to make you realise that you don't have to answer to anybody, that you can be your own boss. You have to want to do whatever you do, every single day. The fact that I was being told, "You have to do this and keep doing it to earn your 50 quid to get your phone" – I think that shaped me, because I didn't want to have to do something that I hated. I think Dad made me work two or three days at first, and when I got that phone, I held onto it like it was a diamond. I never dropped it. I was very careful with it.

Then I began working with my dad properly, being paid for it. I think I got fairly good at painting eventually, despite what my dad and brother Aaron may say, and I'd work between classes, I'd work at weekends. I was earning decent money for my age, while at school and then all through college, and then full time. When I graduated, I went and got the business degree, hung it on the wall, and then picked up the paint brush and went back to work as a means to fund Nutriband, which I had started in my final year.

When I left college, all my friends went into industry, and they started getting their suits and professional jobs. I was coming home with paint all over my face, but the way I was looking at it, I was making the money to start my own business so that I'd never have to answer to anybody again. I spent a couple of years grinding it out. I'd paint all day and then go home, and I'd work on Nutriband in the evenings and during the night.

At first the painting was great for saving for holidays, or lads' trips away or whatever it would be. But as soon as I had the idea for the company, everything just started going into that. I got really obsessed with it. I'd paint as much as I could because I wanted to have the money to buy product, or to have a kitty for travelling to the States when that started.

In my final year at the Dublin Institute of Technology (DIT), I started focusing completely on the company and my college work took a bit of a hit. I thought I was onto the next big thing, and – you know what start-ups are like – I didn't want to tell anybody my idea because I thought everyone would copy it and start their own transdermal patch company and I'd be ruined.

It's kind of silly when I think about it now, because I've since understood how much you need people along the way. I didn't tell anybody what I was up to, but I was working on it so much that I began to miss classes, or I wouldn't show up to projects. That got me a bit of a reputation as a dosser. Classmates didn't want to be with me in group projects because they thought I wouldn't do my part, so I ended up doing a lot of group projects on my own.

But I was just so focused on building up Nutriband that I suppose I wasn't excited to learn things from a book. I was enjoying the process of good and bad, and the experience that I was having with starting the company. I did want to get the degree, because I had put the effort in already, I just didn't have time to study day in and day out, all night long, to get a first. I got a two-two in the end, a very basic business degree, but it was all I needed.

I was looking at the transdermal space on the whole – I had discovered this was the technology behind medical patches. I looked at products that delivered nutrients, which I could start selling to generate revenue and then work towards moving into the pharma field. I was trying to get an understanding on whether patch technology would be accepted for delivering other things besides nicotine. If consumers would happily take their vitamins in a patch for example, then they would likely take their medications that way, this was my thinking.

My research had led me to a Chinese manufacturer who could coat patch products, so I was in regular contact with them, asking whether they could make this or that patch. I'd sit at home studying molecular weights on certain ingredients, and things like that, at the University of Google, learning how different ingredients react together.

I came up with three very basic vitamin supplement-type products, but I didn't have the means to go and get them tested at a lab. So I just took the hand-written formulations to my local chemist shop. I said, "This is kind of a weird one, I'm sure, but I'm working on creating some products, and I just want you to have a look and tell me if I'm going to kill anyone."

The pharmacist looked at me and said, "Well, I can't go on record or say that it's any good, or whether it's going to work or anything like that."

I said, "Fine, I just want somebody that understands what I'm doing to put my mind at ease." And eventually he confirmed that everything there should be okay, that he didn't see any issues with it.

So I put all the money I had saved into the next step. My parents put twenty thousand euro into it, and this allowed me to start working with the manufacturer in China. Then it was off down to Wexford, to my cousin Alan, an ex-Dub who had moved to Wexford and developed a new accent overnight after touching a hurl for the first time. He is great at graphic design, and using some die cuts we found online, made some very basic packaging. We sent it all off to China with a payment, hoping that they wouldn't just take the money and run! Alan now owns a graphic and video production company called Crannog Films.

Six weeks later there was a shipment waiting for me at Dublin airport, and because transporting the product home from the airport would have cost a couple of grand, we did three or four runs out and back in the family cars, loading up the boxes, driving home, loading up the boxes again. I filled up my mother's dining room with all these boxes from China, with products in them that might or might not sell.

In the meantime, I sent copies of everything to the Irish Medicines Board (now the Irish Health Products Regulatory Authority) and the FSAI (Food Safety Authority of Ireland) just to try to get some sort of official certification from them. They came back and said that the products would need to be registered as medical devices and not supplements. This would become very significant later in the story, but I remember thinking at the time – "They are wrong, I'll just sell these as supplements and see what happens." – which was taking a bit of a gamble.

At the same time I went to a Technological University of Dublin (TUD) start-up hub Hot-house, an extension of Enterprise Ireland, looking for financial support, telling them of my plan to eventually move into pharmaceuticals. After a week or so of review they came back and more or less said, "We see what you're trying to do but we don't think it's going to work," after which they went on to list out all the reasons why they didn't think it would work.

I was pretty deflated because that meant I had twenty grand's worth of products sitting in my mother's dining room. I wanted to start preparations towards bringing the products to America. So I started arguing with them. But they wouldn't budge. They told me that the products would already be classed as pharmaceutical in the US, and I didn't have the means to bring them to market. They said "Sorry, nice try. If you think of something else, come back to us, we'd love to work with you." I remember driving home thinking, 'I'll show you this is going to work ...' I nearly put them on the guest list for the NASDAQ bell ringing!

I never thought that the first products were going to be the big game changers. What I wanted was to understand whether people would be open to patch technology for other things beside nicotine. I thought that if people were prepared to take vitamins that way, then maybe they would be open to taking other medications that way as well. That would be a proof of concept, and it would at the same time generate some revenue.

So I got the patch products into a few local mom and pop shops, supplement shops and discount nutrition places, and they were selling one or two boxes a week. My revenues were in the hundreds of euros a year at that point. I then started approaching distributors and found one called WholeFoods Wholesale off the Kylemore Road. When I presented to them, they really liked it, and they said they were going to get it into all the shops. They said to make sure there was a good marketing budget behind it, but that we'd work together and they would work to launch it out, that we were onto something here.

I was thrilled. I was having the very grown-up conversation about what sort of inventory they would want to hold, and what monthly purchase orders we could expect so we could make sure to cover it. WholeFoods estimated we were probably looking at €40,000 a month.

Now I'm 23 at this stage, and this is my business, and I'm on the way. So I went home to try and figure out logistically how to make it all work. I sent through the order for the €40,000 and I think I made €8,000 on that in the end. But the product didn't sell, because of course I didn't have the marketing budget – which I had told them I would have. It just didn't work without it.

I remember following up with them the next month, asking whether they'd be looking to place the next order, and when should I start prepping everything ... They said, "Look, we are not really seeing the run through we thought we would, we realise that the marketing budget isn't there on your side to support it, but we'd be open to selling some of the stock back to you."

It was heartbreaking, because I had pumped the money that I had made from the first order straight back into a second order from China and repeated the process. So it now wasn't just the dining room that was full of product, it was the dining room and half the sitting room as well. My poor mother.

And I had to just take it on the chin, try to keep pushing it in the smaller shops, and hoping that eventually it would sell through and go from there. That never happened. I only dumped a lot of that original inventory as recently as maybe two years ago. I had been holding on to three or four boxes of each product just for nostalgia. It was a deep end learning experience from the business point of view.

This early part of my story was fuelled by naivety and thinking everything was going to go excellently well from start to finish. This was my first experience of it not being the case, and as time went on there would be much worse and more intense experiences on the way to NASDAQ. But that was the first one.

Getting started, I now know you have to use your support network, use people around you, and stop trying to do everything yourself. If you need advice, you have to go to somebody for it and understand that not everybody is looking to steal your ideas. If I could go back and do it again, I would have talked more to people in college about it. I would have talked to more of the professors, people like Tom Cooney, who became very influential in my journey. I would have used my network a bit better, and tried to build it up, and not to think I could wear all the hats all the time. That's the case today. I'm the CEO of the company, but I'm definitely not the smartest person there.

I think I have learned that you have to be prepared to grow slowly, and not to do as I did, to go painting houses for two years and then throw all your money into inventory that you never sell. But if that initial shaping experience hadn't happened, the first NASDAQ refusal and then the second delay would have been more brutal. I'm glad it happened when I look back now.

But I definitely felt very sorry for myself for a while, still selling bits and pieces in the smaller shops, making maybe $60 euro a week, and trying to sell online. I had done things like getting my car wrapped with a logo, trying to look like a big brand, but it never got there.

It wasn't just down to the fact that it was a new product with little marketing spend, it was actually the poor quality of the product itself. There was probably an 18% defect rate on all the products that came from China. Patches that came without any sticking on the back, or patches that came without the right colouring, or completely miscounted – a thirty-pack with twenty patches in it, etc.

More learning! That's something we are so careful with now, we're very detail oriented, whereas I wasn't then, I was just throwing everything at it and hoping it would work out. I was very optimistic about it all.

In February 2025, I was preparing to move back to Ireland with my wife Heidi and our daughter Róe, after eight years in America. As we were packing up our house in Utah, I saw a *Sunday Business Post* article about the company. It made me smile, because it was all about that optimism, that vision. The headline read: *Nutriband's Market Cap Tops $100m After Securing Patent for its Abuse Deterrent Technology*. I thought, "that's what I'm going home to," and it was just brilliant.

Somebody asked me what the headline actually meant, and my answer was that it means the market likes our drive, it likes our confidence, and it reacts well to it, so much so that the stock market is saying we are worth a hundred million dollars. So we are adding claims to our patent, strengthening the case. We filed a continuance, which is technically the issuing of a new patent, and we got a very nice reaction, moving up our stock.

2025 is shaping up to be a great year for us, reaching that market cap, and as I write, we're now closer than ever to file for approval for our first product using our Platfrom technology, AVERSA which will be called AVERSA Fentanyl. This product will be the first and only abuse deterrent product of its kind globally. Independent research has shown that AVERSA could reach peak sales of between $80m and $200m a year, and that could increase substantially if the FDA, after approving AVERSA, were to then decide to mandate that patches must have abuse deterrent properties. Right now and as far as I can see, we are the only company doing this, and this is just product number 1 when it comes to our AVERSA platform.

Our core goal as a company is to change the safety profile of easily abused medications, and make them available to those in need, and we have never been closer to achieving this goal. As I make my home in Ireland once again, with my own family, I'll be looking forward to achieving that goal with Nutriband, to all the ways I can get stuck in to life here once again, but I'll also be looking back now and then, wondering how it all actually happened.

2: Nutriband Beginnings

If I were to put the success of my business down to one thing, it would be the way that I grew personally, arriving at a mindset where I could appreciate that not everybody was trying to steal my idea, and that I simply couldn't do it by myself. You need to surround yourself with the right people.

Right now, while I'm one of the largest shareholders, I'm not the highest paid person in the company. I made sure that Alan Smith, who's our chief Operating Officer and lead Scientist, is paid the most in the company because, in my opinion, there is no company without him. He needs to be cherished and feel appreciated.

It's a maturity thing that came gradually, and it was very difficult to learn and accept. But then I started to see the benefits of it. To think I spent nearly four years not telling anybody what I was doing, trying to do it myself, and going nowhere except for winning a few startup awards. Yet when I started to branch out and talk to people, and establish a network, a few years later we're a NASDAQ application!

There is also an understanding, maybe, that the initial product or idea is only a trigger, because essentially the game is not about the idea; the game is about the strategy, the growth, the development, the vision.

I probably realised this around the time that I had my first negative experience with an acquisition that went badly wrong, and I recalibrated my whole approach to how I sought advice from people with experience.

Then you grow in confidence, and you start to talk a little bit more – it's not just this idea, there is a bigger goal. You start to feel comfortable talking about the big picture, and not being worried that people are going to say, "Thanks for the idea, see you later kid ..."

It was a gradual thing. It took me years to get comfortable initially, and then far less time to get very, very comfortable talking about it. And then it builds to – "Who can I tell now about it? Who can we bring in that will be beneficial?" But it also helps that we have protections in place at this stage, we have intellectual property locked in all over the world.

You need exposure, you need to be loud, you need to look like you believe in your idea, and you don't need to be the shy guy in the corner, working on something that really isn't materializing.

This story is my entire CV. This is my entire work experience, starting in college and going from there, riddled with naivety at first, then when everything started going pear-shaped, growing up fast and learning to rely on people. At this point I would say I have surrounded myself with the best people in their position in the world for what we're trying to do.

I've been lucky to be able to do that, and I think you have to acknowledge luck as well – those chance moments that lead to something big. If I had never taken a rainy Tuesday night meeting in Dublin with an eccentric older lady called Dina, I wouldn't be where I am today. If that hadn't led to a weekend in Vegas in order to meet up with Serguei Melnik, my business partner, we wouldn't have formulated the bigger vision. I don't know what I would be working on today, but I'm certain I wouldn't be selling two or three boxes of Chinese products a week around Dublin. I might be an accountant or insurance salesman somewhere, wondering whether I should have taken more chances.

One of the very first chances I took was pivoting on my final year college thesis. The more I worked on my patch technology project, the more it looked like a business plan to me. It finally struck me that I should do my thesis on something else and continue this – which I was really passionate about – as an entirely separate endeavour.

Trying to think of something that I could do quickly and easily, I settled on "Corruption In Italian Football". When it was proved in 2006 that Juventus had been fixing matches, they were relegated to Serie B (Italian Division 2) for the first time ever, so there was lots of material available online. So I got a thesis written fairly fast on that subject over the course of a weekend and got back to my business plan.

That's how, in the fourth year of college, the company got underway. I registered a company and – in hindsight – did a lot of things prematurely, because I thought it was a Steve Jobs-level idea. I thought it would change everything – no more needles, no more pills, everyone's going to be using patches for their medications. I just became obsessed with it.

I started researching what could and could not be delivered through patches and then got a bit of a reality check when I saw it wasn't as useful a technology at the time as I was hoping it would be. You couldn't take certain vitamins or medications that way, because the molecule sizes didn't allow the substances to be absorbed through the skin. Theoretically you can now, as it happens, so there's an argument that the idea was somewhat ahead of its time.

The introduction of things like micro needles has changed things. Today we use a dermal ablation technology, which is a fancy word for shooting an electric current into the skin, opening the pores up wide enough to allow ingredients in. Things like that didn't really exist back then, or were only in their early stages of development. They are more prominent now in new product development and clininical development.

But back then, with my possibly ahead-of-its-time idea, I knew this was the thing I was looking for – I was going to be the patch guy. I started working on it pretty intensely, always with that visual of seeing the patch on my dad's arm, and envisioning that transformational moment.

I mentioned that earlier I wasn't the greatest student in the world. In fact, I nearly didn't graduate at all. In our third year, when we were picking our modules, you could go into the marketing group or the accounting group. Of course my entrepreneurial mindset wanted to learn a little bit of each. So I picked mostly the marketing group, but I also wanted to learn taxation, which was a separate module, and there was kind of a technicality that allowed me to do that although it had not been done before.

However, at the end of the year I quickly realised that the classes I had swapped were worth different points. I was ultimately five points short of moving into year four! I kind of just never said anything and DIT never mentioned anything maybe through oversight or maybe trying to ignore the issue like me. So on a technicality, maybe I shouldn't have gone forward, but I did get the degree in the end.

My family lived in Terenure in Dublin on the main road in the village until I was about 7 or 8. Then we moved up the road to Rathfarnham, to a house on a cul-de-sac, where my brother and I could go out and ride bikes and play football and generally drive the neighbours mad.

I'm sorry that my daughter Róe won't get to have that kind of childhood experience, and I often talk to Heidi about it. You know, the freedom of jumping on a bus to Dun Laoghaire, messing around in the Forty Foot, getting the bus home. You couldn't see a 13- or 14-year-old do that sort of thing now.

There was a lovely free element to it with good friends. It's where my business and entrepreneurship started coming out early. One time when I was about 11 I started up a "bike repair shop" because all the kids rode bikes. I set up a stall and if your chain came loose or anything like that, I would charge 50p to fix it. But I spelled the sign 'Bick Repairs.' My parents were going out with a couple of friends that evening and passed by and I could see my dad just looking at the sign and laughing to himself.

Then we set up a football league where all of the different roads in the neighbourhood formed teams and we would play in Castle Park in Rathfarnham. We even got jerseys made! My cousin Tracy's boyfriend at the time, Ronan, worked for a company called Azurri where we got them done. We called ourselves The Brookvale Rovers. I loved the organisation and the structure of it all, building something from nothing.

We moved back to Terenure again when I was about 24 and my parents wanted to be back near their friends. It was there that I later crowded out their dining room with boxes.

Dad had inherited his own father's family business, a painting business called Terenure Décor. He was the youngest, and had to take it over, despite the fact that he'd say even today that he didn't particularly want to. But both Dad and Mum were entrepreneurial in their own way. Before we were born, they owned a newsagents on Parkgate Street, and they flipped out of that after four years and bought another shop. Then they went to purchase a pub from the proceeds of that venture, somewhere around the Wexford Street area.

There is a bit of a story to that one. Dad got a phone call from a friend one day who said to him fairly abruptly, "Have you heard?" Dad said, "Heard what?" And the friend said, "Stick on the RTE news." Dad turned it on, and suddenly he was watching the new pub up on the TV screen on fire, so my parents never ended up owning it.

I think years later they got some sort of compensation payment for the deposit or initial investment, but he was gutted.

They bought another shop in Inchicore and flipped it a couple of years later. But they were finished with the shop business at that stage – they'd had enough. My mum went to work for a letting agents – she has always loved the property business – and Dad took the painting back up full time and kicked off Terenure Décor again. That was it for them up until retirement.

I don't know how much money they must have put into Nutriband over the years just to keep it going, or how much belief they held in me, and that it would all work out. I'm sure they must have had loads of reservations that they never told me about. But they backed me, and kept backing me, when others wouldn't. I'm sure they'd invested most of their retirement money by the time we listed, which is a terrifying thought.

Meanwhile, as I mentioned before, the Irish Medicines Board and the Food Safety Board of Ireland (FSAI) were trying to categorise my product as a medical device, when I was placing it in the supplements space. I now know I was wrong, but I was convinced. Looking back, who was I to tell them anything, a complete beginner with a 2.2 college degree. I had written to them for an opinion, saying that all the ingredients I was using were already in protein powders and health supplements, so there was no difference in using a patch for delivery.

They disagreed and said the key word was "ingested." To be considered a supplement, the products had to be ingested. I argued that they were being ingested, just not through the mouth. Their response was that it made no medical sense whatsoever, and that this was not how the law was written.

It went back and forth. They said it didn't matter what I thought, or whether I disagreed, that this was the opinion they were giving. I remember getting really annoyed and sending in the Oxford English Dictionary definition for the word "ingested," which was just: "something that is absorbed by the body". So how could this possibly be a problem?

The woman I was dealing with eventually told me that she didn't have to explain anything to me, that it was what it was. But I wasn't taking no, and I kept arguing, right to the point where I was eventually introduced to the Director of Scientific Affairs, who actually tended to somewhat agree with me in the end. He told me he saw where I was coming from, and that while he didn't necessarily think I was a hundred per cent wrong, with the way these things are controlled and accounted for, that was just how it had to be.

I still argued that they couldn't rewrite the English language to fit what they wanted it to be. That I was going by the official definition, and this is how it should work.

Eventually I got a letter from him stating that they were basically okay for the products to be marketed, so long as there were no adverse reactions. He advised that I go back to the FSAI and notify them that I intended to follow all applicable supplement laws. And that letter was very, very useful down the line with our SEC investigation, because it was used as something that we relied on in good faith.

At this time I had the products in smaller shops around the place and was selling them as a means of getting a little bit of income. I wasn't really making much on it, it was only a couple of boxes a week, but it still felt nice that those couple of boxes were actually selling. Every so often I'd get a website order, but even then, I was trying to ramp things up.

Pretty soon I began working online with a company based out of Utah who had taken an interest in what I was trying to do. It was called "Nutranomics," and it was run by a guy called Tracy, who had a reputation as a bit of a mad scientist. I still have a great relationship with Tracy today and he's one of the best formulators I think I have ever met in the neutraceutical and supplement space. I began working with him because he liked the idea of what I was trying to do, which was formulating products and making supplements. A big part of his market was in Asia, to where he was exporting from Utah.

I had been seeing a girl at the time who had introduced me to her uncle, who seemed to know a lot of people in the space, and he introduced me to a man called Michael, who for a couple of years early on became something of a mentor. Michael told me about this wacky scientist kind of guy he knew, who'd come up with some innovative products, who had a big foothold in Asia and that it might be worth having a conversation with him.

After talking online with Tracy quite a few times about the products, and about the idea of using transdermal tech in a wider way, it got to a point where we were both keen to sit down and see what we could do together. So I began flying to Utah at that point, to meet with Tracy to strategise and work on the products. It definitely wasn't flying first class or anything – it was just about manageable. My parents helped out every so often, and I also had a friend who worked for Delta, who was able to give me a buddy pass now and then, so I could fly for free, and that helped a lot.

I tried to go for about three weeks at a time, so we could get stuck into the work. We were working on lots of ideas and products and sending samples to Asia. We also were working with a guy from Korea called Steve, which I'm sure wasn't his given name, and he was very confident that we could launch a brand and products into Asia.

The idea of Asia was interesting because I was running out of steam in Ireland. I had pitched my idea to Enterprise Ireland (EI) in my final year, but was more or less told that it was never going to work, "and here are the reasons why..." I hadn't accepted any of those reasons. I thought that for every reason mentioned, there must be a solution.

In fact, I felt that their job should have been to help navigate solutions, not just put up a brick wall. So I was quite annoyed for a time. I'm well over it now, and I don't have anything against them. I think they do great things. But it was probably a blessing in disguise that they weren't interested, because if they had become involved, they would now probably own about 10% of the company.

But still at the time, it was quite challenging to have an organisation of authority like that tell you your idea is never going to work, forget about America, try something else. I have an email from them that basically said, good lad, keep at it, and let us know when you have your next idea.

I know now that I quite like being told things are ridiculous, or impossible, or not achievable, and then taking a crack at it and making it happen. But at the time it was a real set back, coming on the back of a different kind of success, the student or start-up award circuit.

2014 was the year of the awards. I was still in Ireland, going to Utah when I could, and in the early days of the relationship with Tracy. I began to focus on awards because they came with prize money and that helped take that pressure off.

So I submitted my project for Ireland's Best Young Entrepreneur competition (IBYE) – entering at local enterprise level to begin with, and then it went on to regional finals where I was eliminated. Not making it to the National final was a tough one to take at the time. I was South Dublin's Local Enterprise Office entry, and I remember getting the call that I'd been shortlisted for 'Best Established' business, which I thought was reaching a bit, because it was so early.

But I did in fact win the "Best Established" category for South Dublin, and then it went into a pot with the best new idea and the best start up to represent South Dublin. I won the South Dublin Best Young Entrepreneur as a whole at that point.

Unfortunately for me, the best start-up, which I had just beaten in the South Dublin phase, went on to win the national competition. It took me a long time to get over that one! And to rub it in, they won €100,000! In the end I got a €20,000 prize from the South Dublin round and that helped a lot. It funded things for the better part of a year.

Actually I got great support from the South Dublin Local Enterprise Office (LEO). A woman called Ena Coleman was assigned to my application for funding from them. She really challenged me early on – questioned it and made me qualify why I thought it was a runner. I like working in that environment where they're stress-testing the idea. She was even questioning why, if EI had said no, she should take the gamble? She more or less told me it was high risk, and for a couple of weeks we were back and forth, she kept asking for more information and I kept presenting the idea and the plan over and over. Eventually she gave it the green light.

That came with some financial support, a third of which was going to be repayable. So it gave us some more finance on top of the awards that we'd already won. I think it was in the region of €15,000, which was a huge amount at the time.

The awards were a great way of funding the business, building awareness of it and getting coverage in the papers. So I did the Bank of Ireland Start up Awards that year as well, winning the category of Ireland's Best New Product and ultimately Bank of Ireland's Best Young Entrepreneur. It wasn't as big a competition, but it came with a lot of press recognition, which was great.

So that was a nice kind of redemption after not winning Ireland's Best Young Entrepreneur competition. I had four awards all of a sudden in 2014 and I could put that on the website. I had leaflets made with all the awards listed there at the bottom. It added tremendous credibility to the products and to what I was doing.

It also helped, in turn, consolidate the relationship with Tracy in Utah. This had become important, because heading into 2015, the fact that we had awards and recognition then attracted the attention of some guys who wanted Tracy to take his company public, with an idea to acquiring us also. They would be acquiring a well-established company which was partnering with an award-winning brand from Ireland that they had potential to develop.

So Tracy got into bed with these people and they convinced him to take his company public. And suddenly he wasn't the CEO anymore, he was relegated to chief formulator or something like that – in his own company. Unfortunately I had been talked into selling my company to them too, as part of the whole thing, to be part of the bigger picture. I did this for five percent, but it was all quickly diluted down to nothing within days.

So there I was in mid 2015, sitting at home in Dublin with a fraction of a percent of a public company that was worth maybe $8 million altogether, because of all the dilution. It was a very daunting moment, and a very steep learning curve on public markets, because I had completely lost control of the company I had built. Even though it was still in its early stages, I'd believed that it could really go somewhere. In hindsight, I think I was all caught up in the travel and the excitement. It was all built on what I thought we could do in Asia with Tracy's connections, but none of that ever materialised.

Tracy and I were both played, if the truth be told. We both fell for the bright lights and the promises in my opinion. It was a public company based in Utah, and they had just listed and were now an OTC company, with great plans to go to a major exchange like NASDAQ or New York. I had sold my company to them for 5% equity in the public company. I was 25 at the time, and the value of the shares I sold had been worth, on paper, a million and a half euro. There was I thinking, "business is easy"!

Then within days they had issued so many shares that my 5% was diluted down to zero point zero zero zero five, the stock price was tumbling and the company was unravelling. It was my first taste of the public side of business, and the sharkiness involved in it all. The whole thing was ultimately a manipulative pump and dump scheme.

By the end of it, when they eventually ran out of runway, they had issued something like eight billion shares before it came crashing down quickly. As of today that company has over 16 billion shares in existence and a stock price of one thousand of one cent per share! This process ensured that a couple of people would make a few hundred thousand dollars and everybody else would be screwed – more on which coming up.

At one stage in the whole thing, they proposed that I should take over as CEO, and put it all to rights for them. And for a very short time I actually thought about it. More naivety!

I talked to people about it, saying, "this is great, I'm going to be the CEO of a public company, I'll have a window office – I'll be running things – I can turn it around and put the patches back to the forefront." I loved the idea, and got really excited about it. But then I found that I just couldn't make myself send back the email to accept the offer. My gut was telling me, "Something is not as it seems, something stinks here," and thankfully I made the right decision. Had I been at the helm when it all came crashing down my name would have been ruined in this industry.

It was a bad experience, but I learned a lot about what not to do directly from it. If they had not been greedy, and not gone into it for a quick dollar, that company would still probably be listed today and be at a decent value and everybody could be happy. But with a public company either one person makes a million or two very quickly, and everyone else loses badly, or quite a few people can make many millions a few years later.

It takes a lot of trust and a strong will to go through that. Take the relationship I have with Serguei, my business partner for the last 10 years. At any point in time, one of us could have screwed the other over entirely and left him with nothing. If I were to dump my shares today, I would make enough money to retire and Serguei and the rest of the team would go away with 20 cents a share – and vice versa, if Serguei was to do the same. So you have to be very careful, and very lucky, with the people you work with in this kind of industry.

It brought me back to the time when I first began talking about focusing on America. Professor Tom

Cooney told me, "be careful over there. They're all sharks – they are not your friends." I brushed it off, saying, "you don't know them like I do, I have deals on the table ..." And then the first chance they were given, they did the worst thing possible. I was left sitting at home with all these awards on the mantelpiece and not a company to my name, which wasn't a good feeling.

The interesting thing with Tom Cooney is that we didn't really develop any sort of relationship until after I left college. I wasn't a star student or anything like that. I did enjoy his class, it was interactive and interesting and was never an *open your books on page 48* kind of thing. He used to bring entrepreneurs in to speak, which made it interesting, and another thing he did was to put people into groups to come up with a business idea and pitch it back to the class. I never got called to pitch, so that tells you something. I was very much a backbencher, but I enjoyed it. It's probably the only class that I remember going to with any sort of enthusiasm.

In 2014 when we won those awards, he invited me to speak at his class, and I have been back almost every year since. That was a nice turn of events, going from a very forgettable student, I would say, to that position where I was an entrepreneur telling my story to a class of students. I kept him up to date on how things were developing, and later he became a member of our advisory board.

I think he liked the fact that my conversations with him have never been straightforward. They probably left him wondering what I was smoking after we'd had the conversation, some of the ideas were so out there. But it's nice to have somebody who keeps you grounded and keeps you level, yet at the same time doesn't clip you. For instance, if you have a big dream or a big desire for what you're trying to do, he'll be your number one advocate so long as you can reasonably qualify where your head is at. He tells you to be careful, to be wary, to keep your wits about you, but never tells you not to do it, or that it wouldn't work.

Serguei Melnik has the same sort of mindset. He was the one who pushed me to eventually go and get my company back. And I only met him because of one of those random life-changing moments that veer between luck and fate. I mentioned my friend whose uncle was well connected and good at putting me in touch with people. Well, he called me one night to say that a friend of his was flying to Ukraine, with a long layover in Dublin. Suggested it might be worth having a chat with her, although he didn't know whether anything would come from it. But since the layover was something like eight hours, he figured she'd probably be happy with a meet up and chat to fill the time.

It was a filthy wet Tuesday night in Dublin, it was freezing outside, the traffic was mad, I was sitting at home, good and comfortable, and was in no mood to go out. So I very nearly didn't. Then something said *just go, you don't know what's going to come from it.* And so I pulled myself up and forced myself to go out. It turned out she was a very eccentric older lady called Dina Lyskovetz who made a lot of money out of True Religion jeans. She was obviously fond of younger men, and was kind of flirty and funny, but it was a good meeting, and she became a great advocate for us, and that's what I mean by making your luck. It was Dina who introduced me to Serguei!

Had I not taken that meeting, I would never have met Serguei, we would have never come up with our plans, and things would never have taken the trajectory they did, because I was so close to not going out that night and meeting with Dina.

I had a Skype call with Serguei after Dina made the introduction. When I was telling him about the company, I remember, for whatever reason, that he took the phone call facing to one side – so I just remember the side of his face. It was like he was on his computer looking at his screen as well as being on our call on his phone. I remember him saying that my idea was very interesting, that he thought we could do something with it. We started formulating the idea of listing on the OTC first (even though we had no right being a public company), so that instead of raising expensive money, we can use stock to start purchasing smaller companies and build satellites around us.

Serguei has been extremely influential in getting the company to where it is today. When we eventually met, we had this similar feeling about its potential and we shared a vision about how to go about it. Our mindset was that if we were going to do it, we should just do it. And we didn't want to build something comfortable, we knew we should build something *big*. We shared that same approach. Had I met somebody who didn't share that, maybe the company would still be an Irish regional start-up.

We decided we were going OTC, and we were going NASDAQ. That was the journey. The method was that we would find a way to use stock as an acquisition currency in place of cash. But first I had to get my company back.

3: Sliding Doors

The people who support you and believe in you, the people who go through all the ups and downs with you, are just so important, even when they don't fully understand what you are doing or why you are doing it. I don't know how many times I had a conversation with my parents saying, "we're nearly there, success is just around the corner, but can you help out with rent this month?" The actuality of it was that we were *nearly* a multi-million dollar company, but in the meantime, I wasn't quite making it to end of the month, so I'd often have to ask them for a couple of hundred euro. Then I'd promise to send it straight back, but of course but they never looked for it.

I have paid them back many times over by now, and I have given them shares in the company that today are worth quite a lot. And that's a really nice feeling for me. They must have had many worried conversations with each other over the years without my knowing about it, but they never once told me it was time to come home and put my degree to work, that it was time to become an accountant. I could sense how much they were feeling for me as time passed. One of the hardest things – and

I have always described the feeling as something that I've never had before nor want to have again – was when we got our first rejection from NASDAQ. All the phone calls I had to make, breaking it to people, knowing that it was going to be at least another year of tough times, and driving an Uber so we could eat and make rent.

When I was going over and back to Utah at the start, one of the first friends I made was Kevin Kostenborder and on Saint Patrick's weekend in 2015, we decided to go to a bar called Gracie's, in downtown Salt Lake City. We were having a couple of drinks when I saw this beautiful girl with blue hair.

I remember turning to Kevin and saying, "the girl with the blue hair down there is pretty smoking, we need to go over and hang out." Now I don't know how positively this paints me, but my idea was to get Kevin to talk to her, and I'd go and talk to her friend, because I wanted her to wonder why I wasn't talking to her.

So we introduced ourselves and Kevin started talking to Heidi and I was talking to her friend. Right at the very end, just as we were leaving, I asked for Heidi's number, and she said yes! When I eventually met up with Heidi, I had to admit that there had been a game plan all along. It was a bit of a gamble; she might have taken offence at me apparently trying to hit on her friend. But she clearly didn't, because we are still here.

Heidi bought into the whole story pretty well and has stuck with me throughout. Later, when we lived in Ohio, she worked as a nanny for a very wealthy family, and how do I put this delicately – the two kids were very difficult and wild, that's the only way to describe it. One day during the summer when she was minding them, the six-year-old chased Heidi around the house lobbing apples at her head and threw an apple right at her face. She came home from work that day with a mark on her cheek.

I remember telling her, "you know, don't worry about it, we're going to do really well, and when everything happens, we're going to be so well off, you won't have to work for people like that." And there she was, with a massive apple-shaped mark on the side of her face.

I don't know how she dealt with it all, to be honest, all the stops and starts. She says today that she never doubted me. She is either the most loyal person I have ever met or the best liar I have ever met. I think she learned to adapt to all sorts of things during all the hardships and it has made her so much stronger. Heidi has always been a hard worker and would get stuck in to help us earn an income, but the constant inconsistencies of where we lived etc left her picking up jobs like nannying rather than anything she could put her degree to. She sacrificed a lot on our journey together.

But back in 2015, I was now spending more and more time in Utah, because of the incentive of seeing Heidi as well as working on the business and having strategic Skype calls with Serguei.

Serguei and I met in person for the first time that Thanksgiving in Las Vegas, after a meeting was set up by Dina. Heidi, whom I'd been seeing for a couple of months at this stage, came with me from Utah for the road trip and the Vegas weekend, so she was there right from the start.

We drove to Vegas, because it was cheaper than flying, a six hour drive. We met with Dina the night before, and she told us a bit about Serguei, and reminded us why she was introducing us to him. Then the next morning, we all met in the Starbucks at the Luxor Hotel, did our intros, and then Dina poured a naggin of vodka into her coffee cup, to get her going. She always had a little flask with her. I remember Serguei saying, Dina, its eight o'clock in the morning! And then Dina said, well, we're Russian I mean, what's the problem? And there was just kind of a comical silence at the table as Dina tucked into her Smirnoff latté.

My first impression of Serguei was that hey, this guy is jacked up, a bit of a strong man build. I was very into fitness and the gym myself at that time, and he had these arms bursting out of his shirt. I mean, you wouldn't take him on at arm wrestling.

We talked for a few hours in the Starbucks and then carried on in his very fancy suite – we were staying in the back corner of the Luxor, down by the kitchen – and we hit it off very quickly. It was a great meeting, very direct and straightforward, no one putting on a mask. It was straight to the point about the opportunity, which we all agreed was there. We started mapping things out, planning it out, and later that evening talked it all through again over dinner. We all left Vegas the next day with mild hangovers, but feeling really good at what was ahead.

As I got to know Serguei I realised he has a short fuse, but has a great heart. He has that very Eastern European demeanour – and if it's fair to say – there's a reason why they were always the James Bond villains! He is from the former USSR, and that's very complicated for him, particularly with issues like we see in Ukraine today.

He's the very best host I have ever met. Later, on visits to his home in Florida, I saw that he would do anything for you. The food, the hospitality, the welcome – that's very much their culture. There's always something planned for you, VIP passes to Disneyland, trips and outings. When we barely knew him, he gave us the keys to his car to go and explore Orlando. He throws a locally famous Halloween party every year. That's who he is.

We often joke now about his temper, which we have rebranded as his 'passion'. And I can say there have been plenty of passionate encounters and conversations along the Nutriband Journey.

In yet another one of those weird sliding doors moments, Serguei almost didn't go to the meeting for family reasons. He used to go scuba diving with friends every year at that time, to avoid Thanksgiving. He says he hates the bland, undercooked turkey favoured by his in-laws. Don't tell them I said that, I have heard it has actually improved quite a lot since then! But for whatever reason, he decided not to scuba dive that one time. He had a feeling he should come to Vegas, meet me in person, and get cracking on the plan if that was what we were going to do.

Afterwards he said he was really torn, and didn't know whether he was making the right decision, because he was letting his friends down, and the scuba trips were a lot of fun. But in the end, he didn't want to pass on the opportunity for us to sit down in person. And it was lucky he did, because two months later we were absolutely clear on our strategy and we had filed our Form 10 to list the company on the public markets.

In our calls prior to this, I had told him what had happened with Nutranomics and he had really pushed me to get my company back. I remember trying to convince myself that it was not that big a deal, that we could just do the same thing under a different name.

"No, it is a big deal," he told me. "We have to get it back. We have to keep the Nutriband name. This is the name that has the awards, this is the name that people think of when they think of you. You can't start over again and just call it Sheridan Patches. You need to go get your baby back."

By this time, a new CEO had been appointed to take over the mess at Neutranomics, and Serguei suggested I get in front of him and explain what happened. He reasoned that as there were regulatory issues involved, no one would want the attention or the media noise.

So I reached out to the CEO and suggested the reasonable approach. I said that we could do this in an amicable way and avoid litigation, that we didn't have to get lawyers involved. It took a bit of doing, but I must have got him on a good day, because he agreed to sign everything back over, so that deal effectively never happened.

It was very quick. Done and dusted in a matter of days – a piece of paper signed and that was it. There was no back and forth, there was no long, drawn out legal expenses. It was a simple recission of the agreement and here you go, let's move on from here. As I said, I think I got him on a good day, it was just great. I later found out that he was quite a colourful character, involved in quite a few questionable ventures, so we had a lucky escape.

After that experience, I now know I know to do the research carefully, to search for people online, to do whatever background checks are necessary before making major decisions, or entering partnerships, because you can't be too careful. But at the time, believe it or not, I was suggesting to the CEO that maybe we would work together in the future, to get the conversation going!

It turns out this gentleman, the CEO, was a rich medical professional living in Park City, Utah, where the Sundance film festival is held and where the celebrities have their winter ski homes. I found reports in the local media of people saying he'd ruined their lives through deliberate malpractice, doing surgeries they later claimed they didn't need and the like. I couldn't believe what I was reading. And then there was a PBS news report that linked him to a romantic scam, where he convinced a woman he was seeing to invest her life savings and retirement money in a Nigerian gold mine. A bit like the emails you get from the African prince, she was going to get ten times the return on her investment, and they would retire on a luxury yacht together.

Well, whatever I said in my original conversations with him about working together, obviously that never happened. He actually only stopped reaching out to me maybe two or three years ago, asking me to work with him on some new start up or other, one of them a liquid marijuana project ...

Getting the company back was a key part of the Las Vegas dinner conversation. So were initial plans for where we could take the company afterwards. We discussed devising a strategy to take it into the Pharma space and go way beyond what it was achieving at the time, which was minor sales in small supplement shops.

We tossed around what we would need, which people we would need, and what companies we could buy to ramp up the growth. As we started thinking about it that way, I knew this was exactly what I'd had in mind – to find the perfect business partner. Serguei was it for me, because we were so aligned on how to go forward which I think is pretty rare.

Serguei's experience was in capital markets. He had worked on taking a number of companies public before and had advised several other companies on going public. His biggest one was a European wine company which he had taken public on the Amex in 2003, and on which he had gotten badly burned. So, on his end too, finding that person, that partner to work with who isn't going to take advantage of him, was now a key driver for him.

According to Serguei, the irony was that this wine company had been a perfect opportunity. Had the two owners not been greedy, it would likely still be listed today, and probably worth a small fortune. They owned a big vineyard and a hefty chunk of the wine production in the country where it was located, a big wine producing country. So with Serguei's help and advice, they listed in 2003. Serguei had been hired on as the Chief Operating Officer by this point. But then a year or so later, Serguei was taken back by the lack of growth in the company's value and he was not receiving stock reports as was the norm, which he had found strange. Other small issues started to creep in then like not being paid correctly and agreements not being kept.

After expressing his concerns, the owners offered him a deal. They said if he could grow the company and get the stock priced above $5 a share as a result, they would pay him everything that he was owed, all backdated.

He thought he'd work to build awareness, he'd put a marketing campaign in place, bring in new institutions, attract strong investors. He couldn't promise $5 a share but he put the plan into action, giving it his best shot. And then he began watching the market, and every time it would hit $5 a share, after all his work, it would fall back down again, under $5 – it never held. Clearly what was happening was that every time it got to $5, the owners sold more shares, and it would fall right back again.

At one stage they stopped paying the bills, and he had to put in $15,000 of his own money to cover the listing fee for that year to try to keep the company listed on AMEX. He had his own shares in the venture at the time too, so on paper he was worth a couple of million dollars, and he was still a very young man on that project. One day he noted that all the stock reports for many months arrived to his office all at once, as if they were being held from him and when he saw the owners had been consistently selling stock under his nose he quit that same day.

The stock took a 50% dive on the announcement of his resignation in fact, and he sold his shares for pennies on what could have been dollars in the end. Not long after that, the company got de-listed for not paying their AMEX listing fee – presumably because Serguei was not there to cover it that time round. I remember him describing these guys as people who believed they were more valuable when they owed money, since they held the cards, without realising that the AMEX or any stock exchange just doesn't play those games. If you don't want to pay your membership fee, then ... see you later.

The learning curve for him was that he realised he was working with people who just didn't understand the value of what they had, or what it could be. The company was just something they were going to tap and tap and tap until there was nothing left. He still talks about it, heartbroken that the people who owned the business didn't understand the fundamentals. If they had, it would have a huge value today.

In terms of Nutriband, our assets were clearly not going to be vineyards or valuable bottles of wine, they were of the Intellectual Property (IP) type, but not yet in terms of patents. At that time, you couldn't even call it a trade secret, it was more like a trade idea. It was where we saw the transdermal industry going, the vision, what we could build it into, and the IP we could develop.

In reality, we had very little. So if we were to try to raise money, it would be very expensive. If we were to try to do an angel round, we'd give away half the company. So instead we thought, why not take Serguei's capital markets experience and my own knowledge of the company and the industry, and go ahead and list on the OTC market? It wouldn't be ideal, but it would give us a trading stock that we could use in place of cash, and then we could purchase smaller companies with technologies that interested us, but also companies that didn't have the means themselves to develop any further. It made complete sense to us.

So we filed a Form 10 to list on the Over The Counter markets with the Securities and Exchange Commission that January. It was only two months after formulating the plan and we had no real resources, but we had found an investor – who is a shareholder today – whom we convinced to give us $100,000 for the project. And that was more money than I had seen in my life up to that point.

I think it's fair to say that Serguei liked my ambition and drive as much as I liked his, because really there wasn't a whole lot else there. It was an idea, and it was a couple of boxes in my mother's front room, and some questionable Chinese products. But it was the idea of potential growth, I think, that got us both excited – as well as the size and scale of where we thought we could take it.

I think he enjoyed the story too, and the challenge of it all. Getting the company back was a big win, obviously, and he was quite excited that I achieved that, on his encouragement.

The Nutranomics experience, in hindsight, was not all bad. Tracy definitely fine-tuned the formulations we had. We had better, sleeker packaging from Korea. Tracy had put his stamp on it and put the right people around it to take my makeshift version, and make it look like something you could see and buy on the shelf. So we took that away with us. But ultimately, those types of products are what landed us in serious trouble with the SEC, a major hurdle in a long line of them.

We were doing patches, with a view to quickly moving into the Pharma space. We thought we would potentially keep these nutraceutical type of products, but we knew we wanted the focus to be Pharma and prescription patch technology, building and scaling companies to get there. With our Asian connections established, we could sell products in Asia and still try and promote and sell them in America for cashflow to fund the company.

But let's talk about the OTC market for a bit, the kind of products that are traded there and how it all works. I don't want to say that it is less regulated, but the OTC market is basically for stocks that trade on a non-major exchange. It's broken down into a number of sections, and they have tried to improve the regulation in recent years. But it's always going to have that reputation for being a place where pump and dump schemes can happen, involving "Wolf of Wall Street" type stocks.

Basically, you have "pink sheet" stocks that trade through an over the counter market as opposed to a major exchange like the NYSE or the NASDAQ. They're really the bottom of the barrel, and they don't even require to be adequately filed with the SEC. These companies can say they have done a million dollars in sales, and it's really some guy sitting in his basement. It's trading speculatively. You trade them with money that you're ready to lose. You might make some more, you might do OK, but for the most part it is cowboy country.

Then you have OTC or over the counter trading. That's split into regular OTC stocks, and they've now added the categories OTC-QB and OTC-QX, which are more for companies that have the potential to reach a major exchange like New York or NASDAQ. But they are still OTC, and it doesn't matter if it is QX or QB, many would say they still have that negative connotation.

In QX and QB you have to meet certain shareholder equity, revenues, and standards, so that's why they have broken it down, and they try to use those QB and QXs to validate companies that are trading on the OTC, because they are SEC reporting companies, and they do have to file sufficiently. QB is a slightly lower tier than QX. QX are usually trying to graduate to the New York or NASDAQ. They are the sort of companies whose fundamentals are getting close to allowing them to list on a major exchange. But you also pay for that privilege.

QX costs about $20,000 a year to list, QB costs around $14,000 a year. We stayed on QB because really didn't see any benefit in graduating from one to the other. We knew we didn't want to be a regular OTC, we wanted some sort of differentiator, but then we were always aiming for the NASDAQ. You can go up through the ranks from pink sheet to QB to QX and then to full listing. That's how they try to structure it. But you can also go straight in to QB or QX. And in reality, very few companies successfully up-list from an OTC, whether you were previously QB or QX.

The other issue is liquidity. A lot of major funds can't touch OTC companies, so you can't attract the big funds. No reputable money will trade OTC stock. Those people trading OTC stock are often kids that are getting into stocks with their allowance – or you're being traded by guys that are probably deliberately trying to pump up your stock. So for us, it was always only a stepping stone.

I can give you an example of the kind of disreputable trading that goes on. A person we knew was a shareholder in a particular company in 2020, and asked us what we thought of it. The company was claiming they had a cure for Covid, and the stock went from something like 10 cents to $40 in a very short space of time, so that the company was suddenly worth a billion and a half. I was looking at their SEC filings and they literally had four grand in assets. They had no sales. It looked like their filings were written by a twelve year old.

Serguei told this guy straight away, that this was an absolute scam. We told him to take whatever was left of his money and run away from it as fast as he could, not to try to get people to invest, not to take a role with the company, because he would get in trouble for even being associated with them or having any kind of relationship there. I remember thinking that I wouldn't even touch this with a barge pole. But he wouldn't listen. He said, "They're doing great things – they have a cure for Covid!" I mean, sure. A random company in Kansas had just cured Covid, and AstraZeneca hasn't got there yet!

So, we did warn this person. Serguei assured him that he'd been in capital markets for twenty years, and he'd never seen such a delusional trap for anybody who was involved in this company. It was only a matter of time before regulators came knocking.

But they ended up joining the company, putting up posts about it and enticing friends, family, and other shareholders to get involved and invest. Then the SEC sued them, the FBI ended up getting involved, and there are individuals right now in prison as a result.

So the pink sheets layer of the market is not regulated at all. Technically, if you are on the OTC, you have to be an SEC-reporting company, you have to have an auditor, you have to pay your fees. But it is easily manipulated, because most of the stocks are low volume. So you'll have companies whose sole job is to pump up a stock by sending email blasts to 100,000 people in the hopes that people will buy it, meanwhile these same companies will have bought your stock and then sell at the top after luring investors in.

You'll see OTC stocks that will be $2 one day, $50 another day, $12 the next. I can't imagine the amount of people that are being scammed and are losing money just from email blasts or cold calls from modern day boiler-rooms, which are rampant. These will be run by very loosely qualified dealers from some okey dokey brokerage in Boca Raton, Florida, and they'll be getting up to all kinds of dodgy things. We've been approached by them before, and have told them straight up that we won't work with them.

They say things like, "We can improve the value of your stock." Really? How, exactly? How can anyone except us increase our own value through hard work, acquisitions, strategy and all the rest of it. No one else can do it for you. How can someone else possibly build a value in your company without something meaningful or fundamental to base it on?

We didn't want cold calling, we didn't want email blasts. Sure, we wanted awareness and visibility, but we don't want a broker that's calling and pressuring 75-year-old people to invest their retirement money. That's the difference, I think, with the OTC and what we have.

The other thing I've noticed is that brokers will get a kick back on stock sales. So they'll get a target, say a $10,000 investment for a particular company today, and they'll get a 20% bonus on that. It's completely illegal, but it goes on. They'll sell you the moon and stars, get their commission, and move on. Then all of a sudden somebody who's invested has lost 80% of their money and they can't even get a call back. So we've been very particular about companies we do and don't work with – we've only ever worked with reputable companies.

I get cold calls, even currently, asking what I think about this or that investment opportunity. I just don't even engage, because I don't want there to be a record down the line, when an investigation starts. If the FBI are going through that company's emails, I don't want my email address or my name to come up.

So that's the level it's at. That's what happens in the OTC, whereas it is rare that anything close to it would happen in the NASDAQ. And that's why you get the credibility there. That's where you get a better profile. If your stock is trading at $6 in the NYSE or the NASDAQ, that's because the market has put it there, not because some guy in Boca Raton has put it there.

There are reputable versions of getting a hot tip, or hearing about a hot stock to watch for. It could come from an analyst who has genuinely researched that company, believes that it is the next big stock, and puts out a release on that.

They'll very clearly have a disclaimer at the beginning that says, this is not investment advice, it's an opinion piece, so they protect themselves immediately. But you know, if you get a random email from George Gonzales in South Florida that says, "Don't tell anybody, but this stock's going to $100, invest now," that's a problem. We have an analyst from Noble Capital now who's covering us, and recently they put out a report on us with a price target. But that's a reputable price target from a reputable bank and analyst. If www.nextbighotstock.com sends you a tip, its usually not reputable.

So you have to ask, does it come from an analyst within a bank, and somebody who's been established on the scene, or does it come from a wix website, or somebody that nobody's heard of and who has no following?

This was the world we were diving right into, and though my first taste of public company life with Nutranomics had ended badly, I wasn't put off. It was something I knew I wanted. We were filing with the OTC, and as soon as we became effective, we would begin trading.

By the end of 2016 the time had come for me to move to America permanently, so I didn't wait around. I told my folks, this thing has grown legs now, I'm moving to Florida for a while, I need to be there. They said, "we understand, we'll come visit, do what you need to do." And the best part was, Heidi was moving with me.

When I got to Utah, we loaded up a U-Haul, took Heidi's 15 year-old Lexus with 250,000 miles on it, and hauled it across America over four days. We Airbnb'd a house in a nice part of Orlando with a pool, which again, demonstrated a certain naivety. Just because we had filed a Form 10 earlier in the year, I thought we'd be trading stock in a couple of months and I'd be a multi-millionaire in no time.

When you declare effective with the SEC, there are two ways to proceed. One is to raise money, and through your relationship with an investment bank, your attorneys and auditors etc, you can start trading your stock once you're greenlighted by the exchange. The second is that you have to get a market maker to build and develop a market for you. Then you have to get FINRA, the financial regulator, to sign off on the trading of the stock.

All these things were going on in the background, and while we thought it would only take a few weeks, it all got held up again. And now the nice Airbnb and Florida started becoming too expensive, and all of a sudden, we were wondering whether we'd jumped the gun moving there at all.

We couldn't afford to stay in the nice house with the pool anymore, so we got the U-Haul again, loaded her up, and moved to a farm in a place called Deland, which is way out in the boonies, nearly an hour north of Orlando. It was a middle of nowhere kind of place with a lot of pickup trucks and Confederate flags, but we lived in a farmhouse there for another while with the dogs. Months started drifting by and drifting by, and we still hadn't got a trading stock yet.

Then out of the blue, while we were living at the farm, I was contacted by a company called Advanced Health out of Ohio. Dean was the CEO's name, and he had come across our website and liked what we were doing with the patch technology. He said they were working on something similar and there might be some synergies. We chatted for a bit, and he sent me a list of patents that they had, and after looking at them I knew I needed to see more detail on this. I thought this might be just what we were looking for to fit the plan that Serguei and I had formulated, to start buying up these smaller companies with good IP.

I called Serguei to tell him everything I was reading looked really good, that it looked like it fitted what we were trying to do. He suggested we get them on the phone – "Let's find out more." So we spoke to Dean, learned more about his company and asked him to send further details. We needed the actual patent filings – all the details they had so we could do our research. He sent me a list of patent applications that he said they had filed.

Now, everything in there sounded great, and looked great, and you would assume that they had done the relevant work. If a company was being issued patents, you would assume there was some credibility to it. But it turned out it was all smoke, it was nothing, it was just fluff, and it took us a long time to find that out. But at the time I'm saying, "perfect, I'm going to get back to you, there's something we're working on here and we think this could fit the model, this could be a great move for both of us".

A couple of weeks later we put it to him that we would like to acquire them for 5 million shares of the company, which was about 25% at the time. We had since restructured to approximately 11 million shares total. Everybody would maintain their position, it would become a wholly owned subsidiary, so there was no risk of job losses or anything like that, and we agreed verbally to move forward with the deal.

It was around the same time Heidi and I were wondering where we would live next. We had to leave the farmhouse as it had been rented to someone else. We were sitting in a car park one day after getting some groceries. "Will we just move to Ohio?" I said, "Let's just drive to Ohio and we can get stuck in with this new company, and be on the ground and work with them directly."

That was on a Tuesday, and by Thursday the U-Haul was loaded up again and we were back on the road, making the journey up to Ohio where we'd rented another Airbnb. After a day or two we found an apartment. So we were now Ohio residents, living just outside of Columbus, and we had almost formalised our acquisition of the first company in the big scheme.

Not too long before that, I had got to the point where I was running out of visa time, and Heidi and I were trying to work out what to do. We didn't want to separate at that point, and I felt I couldn't leave her there at the farm on her own and fly back to Ireland until I was cleared to come back in six months' time. We even considered both going to Ireland, but what would we do about the dogs?

So there we were just sitting there one evening, working all of this through and we thought, will we get married? Will we just go to Walmart, get some rings and go on to the courthouse? I looked at Heidi and said, "I know I'm in it for the long haul if you are?" And she said, "I'm in it for the long haul too, let's do it!"

So on Friday we did exactly that. We got rings at Walmart, we went to the courthouse in Daytona Beach and got married. It was brilliant, we told nobody. Even my mum only found out a couple of years ago. And Heidi's mom and dad only found out a couple of years after the fact because they noticed on a piece of mail that we were filing taxes jointly as Mr. and Mrs. Sheridan.

As a bonus, I got my Greencard soon after, and that was one less worry for us as a couple, more than anything. We picked up some pizzas on the way home with the last few dollars we had in the bank, and then we were back to trying to figure out where we were going to live, how were going to survive as secret newlyweds.

4: Hauled over the Coals

We ended up spending a year in Ohio working with Dean and the rest of his team from March 2017 to March 2018, and we did finalise the acquisition agreement. But before long certain problems started creeping in. Dean would send me an email saying something like, "we should discuss salaries, I think such and such is a fair amount".

They started pressing for salaries around $250,000 a year at that point and my response was, "sure I'd love that as well, but where do you think the money's coming from? You're aware of our financial situation, this is a bootstrap start-up that you're part of now, and you've got 25% of it. When we list on the NASDAQ later this year, that 25% is going become very valuable."

They went away for a bit, but they'd keep coming back with these complaints that they weren't making money, it wasn't this, it wasn't that... Things were grumbling along like this when one day Serguei called me to say that we'd just got a letter from the SEC, and that they'd started an informal investigation into us.

There were two signatures at the end of the letter. It informed us that they were conducting an investigation into whether any security laws had been broken. They requested that we provide certain information, which we duly sent back to them.

Some time passed, and I realised that Serguei was not really himself, because he knew what this meant. I didn't. He was trying to keep me focused on the business, and unaware of how much trouble we were in.

At this stage we were only pulling something like a couple of hundred dollars a month from the original 100K investment, making it last as long as we could, but one of the things I did buy was a gym membership. I was sitting in the car park at the gym when my phone rang, and it came up as a US government number.

It was the SEC asking me to come in for a deposition the following Tuesday to answer some questions. When the lady on the phone said they were in the Miami office, I replied that to be honest, I didn't think I could afford the flights to get down there. It probably sounded weird, given that we were now a publicly listed company on the OTC. She said, "that's not a problem, we'll cover the cost, just send us your flight and hotel receipts". And that's when I really knew I was in trouble.

When I told Serguei they'd not only called me for a deposition, but that they were going to pay for me to go down there and put me up in a hotel, he was quiet for a minute. Because he had been called too, which meant there was definitely an issue.

Then he began trying to work out what exactly we did wrong that they could have picked up on, because we had been so careful not to do anything stupid. We never did a pump and dump. We never worked with dodgy characters; we never did anything like that. Serguei had seen this kind of inquiry happen before, but usually when a company had done something very obviously wrong.

One of the people we had met through Advanced Health was an attorney called Sharon – quite a stern woman, as many attorneys are. She was looking through everything, but clearly only concerned about the impact on Advanced Health.

She began asking whether there was anything they needed to know. And we said, "Absolutely nothing. We don't know what they're after." But she reinforced what Serguei had said earlier. "Well, if they're paying for you to go down to Miami, they're invested in getting you, you know that?"

At the time of our filings we had received advice from two attorneys and a dermatologist. We had also asked Sharon and another attorney afterwards to look at what was in our periodic fillings. Both had said that as far as they could see, there was nothing in there that we should be worried about.

Serguei was actually deposed first. As a person, a lot of people would consider him hot-headed. But I think he is just passionate about things. If you know him and you understand him, he's a very friendly and considerate person – he wouldn't hurt a fly – but he'll yell when he gets excited or annoyed about something.

He went in without an attorney and, will admit himself, went in kind of cocky on the back of numerous attorneys and a doctor of dermatology telling us we looked fine. He did his deposition, and it all got heated, and at one point, he and the SEC examiner were yelling across the table at each other. Serguei was digging his heels in saying, "We haven't done anything; you haven't got anything on us." And the SEC examiner was saying, "That's for us to decide!" And they were just yelling back and forth.

Afterwards, I called him to ask how did it go, and he said ruefully, "It got quite heated, but look, they're just fishing. There's nothing really specific that they focused on."

He went on to tell me that another of the things they asked him about – and this is so ridiculous – related back to the time when I won all the awards back in Ireland and when I was a Nissan Generation X Ambassador. As part of the role, you had to do video blogs on your company. The SEC had pulled those video blogs, played them to Serguei and were saying, "Is this statement true? Is that statement true? Was he misleading potential investors?"

You know what those video blogs are like. You say we are hoping to launch the products into Asia this year, I'll keep you guys updated, that sort of thing. The SEC said the products never went to Asia. So this was a false statement, and that, "If anyone invested based off this knowledge, they were misled." It was beyond ridiculous.

Then it was my turn and I thought, I'm not going in like this, I need an attorney to go in here, because I've never done anything like this before. They're going to see me as fresh meat, and they're going to know exactly how to play me.

We decided to contact an attorney, Glen, in Florida, whom Serguei knew going back. We had no money to pay him, so we offered him some shares if he came with me. Thankfully he agreed, more as a favour to Serguei than anything else.

On the day there were two guys there, one seemed to be a relatively new or inexperienced investigator. The other was the seasoned head of the enforcement office, a Belgian guy, who turned out to be a bit of a weapon. I remember trying to start the conversation in a light-hearted way. It was around the time of the 2018 World Cup, so I said, "How do you think Belgium are going to do?" He just looked down at me through his thick glasses – completely blanked me, no interaction, nothing.

I was subjected to four hours of questioning. At one point they tried to get me to read out part of a sentence from the filing into the record. I was about to start reading when my attorney told me to stop.

"Get him to read the entire sentence, not just one piece out of context, please."

He was right – the part of the sentence I was reading would have been just awful had you taken it out of context. And you could see the examiner almost smirk a little bit, as if he was thinking, 'so you got what I was doing, I'll allow you that one.' And then it moved on again, relentlessly.

Afterwards Glen said I did well, but that he personally had no idea what they were fishing for. He had not been able to pick up the particular thread they were concerned about, or the particular issue they were basing their investigation on. It was all over the place. He headed to the airport and said to keep him posted on any developments.

As I sat in the hotel that night I tried to persuade myself it was just a formality, that they were just making sure everything was correct. I called Serguei to say, "I think it went okay, I think we're fine."

But then the SEC sent another letter asking specifically about some disclosures we had made on the products. We had previously been advised that they were not due to be regulated by the FDA because they were not a drug, they were not a medical device, they were essentially supplements with a new style of delivery.

It was a bit similar to what I had gone through with the Irish Medicines Board. We had received a legal opinion from Sharon, the Advanced Health attorney at this point. We'd also previously received opinions from the dermatologist and our other attorney – all independent of each other. All confirmed that the statement in our SEC filings was accurate, that it was a legal opinion, and that the advice was to file this with the SEC.

We sent that to the SEC and we didn't hear from them again for some time, until we get a letter back that said, 'we disagree, the products that you are talking about are, from our understanding, medical devices, which would have to follow the supervision and approval of the FDA. We are now going to turn our investigation formal.'

Receiving that letter was like getting a dagger in the gut. It's the only way I can describe it. We were now in a formal investigation with the US government. It was a very, very nervy time for us. The reality, however, is that if you make a mistake in your SEC filings, whether it's a genuine mistake or not, you're deemed liable for somebody potentially losing money if they relied upon that information.

At that same time, we were talking to banks about raising money – possibly prematurely – but we were selling the package of what we were doing. We'd got our first acquisition under our belt, looked at the IP we had in place, and we had filed to get that IP valued, so we could list it as an asset. So the SEC investigation, now formal and serious, was going on in the background and we had to try to have smiley, brave faces while continuing with the plan, and hope that it would all go away.

Despite these problems with the SEC, some good news did come in. The evaluation came back on Dean's IP. The independent view said that the IP in the suite of patents we had would be worth $120 million should the products get to market. It was a great lift, and gave us the feeling that our plan was starting to work, notwithstanding the trouble with the SEC. We had spotted a small company with strong assets and good IP that we had been able to acquire relatively cheaply, and it was now getting a strong valuation.

So I called Dean up. "We got the valuation back on the IP, great news, congratulations, it's at $120 million. This is a big reason to celebrate, go and have a drink." His immediate response was, "Oh man, we sold it to you too cheaply, didn't we?"

That response had great significance. As I said, relations had already become a bit strained, they were constantly asking for more money, and I was completely stretched with the SEC situation. I probably had my eye off the ball. When it came to a routine refiling of the IP, Dean offered to take care of it, only he then refiled everything in his personal name, not in the name of the company. He was possibly hoping we wouldn't notice, that he could hold on to his shares and also hold on to the IP, and then perhaps quietly sell out his shares.

Sure enough, we didn't notice for a couple of months. So we found ourselves about to be sued by the SEC, our IP is locked away, and we're still trying to focus on working with the banks and get all the paperwork ready for a NASDAQ application.

It was around July 2017 that we did our first roadshow in New York. We did the full show, meeting with all the different guys on Wall Street, presenting our case. For me as a relatively recent business graduate, that was just the best two days ever. It was so hectic, but you're in the high rises on Wall Street, you're presenting your company to investment banks – it's just like you see in the movies, and it was amazing. Eventually in 2018, on another follow up roadshow, we settled on Wallach Beth and began moving forward with them. But it wasn't long before it came to the point where I had to come clean with them and say "Look, we have this ongoing situation with the SEC..."

Their first concern was that this would obviously hold things up, so they wanted the name of our lawyer. Thing was, we didn't actually have a dedicated lawyer at this point, we had taken advice from different attorneys along the way, we had a corporate lawyer but not a litigator as well. So they said they would put us in touch with a lawyer who was an SEC specialist, one who knew exactly how to talk their language and play their game. His name was Joe D and he was excellent– he's now a great friend. He's standing right beside us, in our photographs, the day we rang the NASDAQ bell.

Our trouble with the SEC is actually hard to understand, and you try to take the bigger view, in hindsight, and say they are only public servants doing their job and I am a big supporter of why the SEC was established. But I have heard a lot of high profile people question the way they go about it. Anyone who has dealt with the SEC knows how hard it is to get a result. In my opinion, the system is built on attorneys going to work for the SEC and taking on as many easy cases as they can. They build up a name for themselves, then go get hired on a multi-six-figure contract for the law firm representing the exact companies and people they sued while at the SEC. This is not a judgement across the board, but I believe its certainly a flaw in the organisation.

It's kind of a broken system, and you'll rarely find them going after the Bill Gates or Zuckerburgs of the game, or the big guys who have the means to defend themselves. I still think to this day they were under the impression that we would just fold – that we were not in a position to defend ourselves properly.

Yes, we made mistakes, we know that in good faith there were technical errors in a couple of initial filings, but not so much as to put us in the Bernie Madoff category of wrongdoers. The mistakes were in our original filings, and the interpretation of certain products and wether they would need a full Clinical development and FDA approval or not. The saving grace was that our stocks had not traded, and no one had been hurt, or lost any money.

We originally filed our Form 10 with the SEC in January 2016. The Form 10 is your request with the SEC to list your securities for sale on public market. As you know, we didn't have money at the time. Serguei had been burned a couple of times and wasn't flush for cash, and I was driving an Uber.

We knew that the Form 10 could cost tens of thousands dollars to get done. We had money in the bank, thanks to our original investor, our first shareholder, who had believed in our plan. But we couldn't blow it all on a Form 10. That money had to be for operational costs, and needed to last us a long time. So we did the hard yards on drafting the filing ourselves, reading up everything we could get our hands on, and producing the basic document, and then getting our attorney to check through it, beef it up to the standards required and sign off on it, rather than paying attorneys to do all the work line for line, which would have cost us a fortune in hourly rates.

Eventually, we had it all put together, we went ahead and filed, and then sat waiting for a response, full of the hype and the tension. These days, if I were to get a letter from the SEC on a Tuesday, I mightn't read it until Friday. As you mature you realise that it is just an agency, a pain in the ass agency with their paperwork and attention to detail and regulation – no matter how important that work might actually be in the bigger scheme of things.

But we were waiting and waiting, so around a month after we filed our form 10 in February 2016, I called the

SEC examiner and said, "Hello, my name is ..." and I realise my voice is cracking and I probably sound like I'm 15 years old. "Hello ... my name is Gareth Sheridan, and we filed our Form 10 with you a while back? Uh, I just wanted to check on the status ..."

There was silence for a moment, and then a woman's voice just said, "We'll give you an update when we're ready."

I tried to keep going. "Have we a time frame or anything like that?" And again, a flat no. She was just so blunt. I called Serguei, and told him how offhand she'd been.

"She wasn't very pleasant," I said.

"No, this is just how they act," Serguei said. "They take this holier than thou approach, they don't give anything away."

Eventually we received comments from the SEC that we needed to clarify some facts, which we did and sent back. After a while I called again and asked whether there were any updates. It went back and forward like this for a while – she was always pretty cold – but at least she was taking my calls. Finally, one day when I asked if they needed anything else, she said, "No, we don't have any more questions at this time."

So I thought – this is brilliant, we are all set now – good to go! And we declared ourselves effective with the SEC who accepted the declaration filing.

It turns out that 'we don't have any more questions at this time' is not actually a greenlight to finalise and go effective I suppose. I thought we had gone to the end of a process and had come through. How else were we supposed to interpret *no further questions* – a company like ours that was clearly eager to get going, after all the times we had called them? Not to mention they had accepted our request to go effective in our filings.

I think what happened was that the lady we were going back and forth with all the time was quite new and shouldn't have said that to us at all. At one stage, when we were describing what had happened to a supervisor at the SEC, there was a long silence, and then the response, "We're going to have to get back to you on that."

Now I may be wrong, but instinct tells me that the whole SEC investigation that we went through was subsequently a way for them to try and save face about the fact that a new employee verbally greenlit a listing, without any approval from a superior. So they then had to back track, and when the investigation wheels started turning, they had to keep turning. That is the system.

Joe D heard us out when we met with him, and he said it sounded like they were digging their heels in on something. He thought that maybe there was some technicality that they thought they could get us on. "The bottom line now is getting you the best deal we can, and making sure they know that nobody relied on any incorrect information to invest."

When I say the stock was public at this time, it wasn't actually trading, because we hadn't really created a market for it yet. There was no volume on the shares each day. We had a price that had been sitting at $4 since the start, and maybe five or ten shares had traded here and there, but there was no real trading. Joe was convinced this was a big positive, and that the main line of defence we could use was that nobody had lost any money. "I'm going to do you guys a big favour," Joe said. "I know you are not cash-flush, and I appreciate you are a client of Wallach Beth, so I can do this work at a 20% discount, which will be in the region of $700 an hour ..."

And we're thinking, 'Brilliant Joe, thanks for working with us on this,' trying to put on a brave face at the thought of the rate. That's what we were taking in a month from the company! But this was our first big New York law firm and these guys charge the big bucks for a reason. We didn't have a choice. We hired Joe and he started working on it. And as I said earlier, Joe has become a great friend since, and I certainly don't begrudge him his fees. He is worth every cent.

Then the SEC informed that they would be sending us a Wells Notice. A Wells Notice is the formal letter saying why they will be suing you in court and that you have ten days to convince them as to why they should not proceed. So this is now really, really serious, and Joe is going to have his work cut out for him.

At this point we were still working with the banks, who had agreed to proceed with the NASDAQ application in any event. They would put the work in, and we'd all just deal with things as they came along. Apparently, SEC matters are part and parcel of being a public company. They advised us to keep our focus and not to let this steer us off course. This was a big relief. The goal and the model were still progressing. We had issues that we were dealing with, but at least the bank wasn't put off, they were still going to try and get the deal done.

And then by chance I was introduced to a low profile

investor who we can call Dave for the purposes of the book, in Ireland who was interested in investing in the company, which was a real breakthrough. With capital in place, we could defend ourselves, we could keep going, we could focus on the core plans for the company and our NASDAQ listing.

We presented to him, and talked about what we were working on, and described the model, and how we were approaching it. I was convinced that we would have our NASDAQ listing by the end of that year. That's what all the signs were saying, despite the problems, and that's what I genuinely believed at the time.

And that was the sell. "If you come in now, we're trading here today, once we get our NASDAQ listing, we could expect a bump in the stock price and liquidity, and you can exit out of your position and make your return quite quickly."

Dave had just sold a company for about $60 million, and at that meeting, when it seemed he was interested, I remember saying, "So how much will I put you down for?" And he makes a sign for the number 2. I said, "Great, so that's $200 thousand?"

"No," he said, 'I'll go in for two million dollars!"

I was trying to maintain my professionalism, sure thing, let me make a note of that. It ended up being a million and a half – he didn't do the two million in the end – but who's counting. When that came in, it was such perfect timing, since we were running very tight on cash.

Serguei had just put his last savings into the company so we could make a filing, and I had nothing to speak of. I had just sat down with Chase bank. "Look,"

I said, "we just got our IP valued at $120 million and I'm here to see if we can get a loan – a bridging loan to get us to our NASDAQ listing." We needed something like $200,000 at the time. Chase looked at it and responded ... "No, it's not something we can invest in."

We argued that it was independently valued at that, and they still said, "sorry, our guys have looked at this and think it's not something we would be interested in at this time."

In my personal life, about a month beforehand, Heidi and I had realised that we couldn't afford the rent in Ohio anymore. On paper, I was worth something like $8m because I had two million shares in the company. But in reality, we couldn't afford our $1,200 a month rent. It was also around that time when we were starting to fall out with Advanced Health, so we decided just to get back to simplicity and move in with Heidi's parents back in Utah.

We were well-used to loading up the U-Haul by then – I've done that drive across America probably four times at this stage – and we drove from Ohio back to Salt Lake City where we moved into Heidi's parents' basement like a couple of students and faced a complete reset.

Three weeks after that move, Dave's money came in. I remember looking at the Nutriband bank account, which was usually always a red number, a red alignment of numbers, and suddenly it had more zeros than I had ever seen on a bank statement, beyond anything I had ever thought or dreamed of. I called Serguei and said, "the money's in!"

"You're joking," he said, and I said, "no, it's there, we actually have our first big investor." We were both shocked. We knew we had all the paperwork done, and had everything agreed, but there is a part of you that still thinks it is never going to materialise. So this was really, really good. We knew we could get to work properly now.

The first thing we did was to go out and buy new laptops, ones that were actually functional. I was still working off my old Asus from 2010 that kept freezing on me and had no battery life.

We got working and were very careful with that money. We used it to defend ourselves with the SEC. We used it to present in New York. We were focused, and the bank was happy because they understood that people were willing to invest in this company, that it looked strong, and that we'd be able to get the deal done.

But not long after, it was back to reality again. Dean's filing of the IP in his own name came to light just at that time. One of our attorneys brought it to our attention, wanting to know what was going on. We assured him that we'd instructed Dean to file it in the company's name. But now this is a big problem, because our investors thought that we had this IP.

In addition, of course, we now really did have a problem with the SEC, right on the brink of a lawsuit with them. It was not a very pleasant position to be in, and the lawyer said that we needed to contact Dean immediately and threaten that we were going to cancel the acquisition of Advanced Health entirely. So that is what we did.

Advanced had become a huge headache at this point anyway. We sent Dean an email advising that it had come to our attention he had re-filed the IP in his own name, and that as a result we were looking at rescinding the entire acquisition. He wrote back saying something like, "It's not a big deal, we'll just sign another assignment over the IP, it's not a problem."

We responded that was a problem, a big problem. We had disclosures and filings going ahead saying we owned something, when essentially, we didn't, and it was not as easy as just "signing an assignment" again, which we were going to have to publish. It got to the point where our attorneys advised us to rescind the acquisition entirely and move on from them. The deal had gone fully over the line. They had 4.2 million share certificates in their hands. It was done and dusted, and the only way to rescind it and cancel the deal was to sue them for fraud. As it stood, we had nothing, and they had our shares and the IP, and that was what the lawsuit was filed for.

That was another very bad period, and for me, an exercise in growing up very quickly. It was daunting to be in the middle of another form of lawsuit, not just the one with the SEC looming, but a corporate lawsuit, and I certainly wasn't used to it .

Today, if we got a corporate lawsuit – well it's just another day. It's an ongoing thing in this world. In fact, we are in a lawsuit right now with an investment bank with whom we kicked tyres, but never did a deal. They sued us, and when I got that lawsuit, my reaction was, "Okay, we'll counter sue, or we'll see what the advice is ..." You take it in your stride. But back then I was in multiple lawsuits, I was financially struggling, I was worth X on paper and had Y in the bank, and it was a very heavy period of time.

We quickly filed the lawsuit and blindsided them with it. I remember my phone going off and the emails coming in. "I can't believe you did this, blah, blah." I just responded by saying, "Well I can't believe you did that. You gave us no choice. You put back in your own name the one thing we acquired from your company, and then took our shares anyway? What am I supposed to do?"

We filed the lawsuit and a while later, we were called to court, so I flew down to Orlando. We were able to afford attorneys this time, thankfully. Going into the courthouse, we were assured by our lawyers that this was a cut-and-dried case, where there was no way that a judge could look at the facts on hand and not see what we saw. It was Judge Rodriguez presiding, whom we were told went very much by the book – he liked things to be done right, so our counsel was sure he was not going to side with these guys.

Judge Rodriguez starts the trial by saying that this was his last case, and that he wanted to make sure to listen to everything very carefully.

"I don't want a reversal of the decision on my last case as I retire," he concluded. So that was somewhat reassuring to hear.

I went through hours of being deposed and interrogated by their attorneys, and then the next day our attorneys did the reverse with them. Their side was on video camera, not in court. And as I listened, I was thinking how this case was as black and white as it gets, we had nothing and they had everything, how was any judge going to side with them?

At one point the Judge asked Robert, one of the Advanced Health guys, whether he had shares in a brokerage, and a few other things, just simple questions. Robert answered, "Well, uh, uh, I don't really know, um I mean, the IP is there and, you know, we can always just give them the IP ... that's what we're trying to do to settle this case ... We want to just give them back the IP that they bought or whatever, you know, I don't really know what your question is."

The Judge just stopped him and said, "look, age is just a number, just listen to the question and respond accordingly, don't act like you're older than you are."

So we believed that the judge thought that they're playing games, and that he was on to them. We came out of the courthouse after two days with our attorneys smiling and saying, "This went well, we're happy with this."

A few weeks later I was back at the desk back in Utah, when I get an email from our attorney saying, "Good afternoon, with regard to the results of the trial: the Judge found in favour of Advanced."

My first thought was, *did I read that wrong*? I got on to the attorneys saying, "What do you mean he found in favour of Advanced? We walked out of there – you guys said this was as black and white as it gets." And all they could say was that they didn't know what the judge had based this on, that they were really baffled at how he could do that. They told me that they were going to appeal it immediately.

We were absolutely panicked. Now, there was a court order confirming that Advanced had their shares. We were sure they were just going start dumping the stock and flooding the market. We were going to be a five cent stock by the following morning, because they were going to get rid of those shares as quickly as possible before we could appeal it.

But the attorneys pointed out that we had filed an emergency injunction on the shares, so we had a stop on those. Then we called our transfer agent and said by no means at all was he to free up any shares. I told him, "I don't care if you get a legal letter, we'll deal with that, but no way are these shares to be freed up."

So then we went back to the court to file the appeal, which put a stay on any transactions with the stock. But with an appeal you're talking about maybe a year and a half before you get a resolution. So this was something that was going to be hanging over us now for quite some time.

To make matters worse, when we started the action, we'd had to give the court $50,000 as collateral. Judge Rodriguez had not only found against us, but he had awarded our $50,000 to Advanced Health as well. So this gave them $50,000 to use to defend themselves now for the appeal. It was unbelievable. I don't know how else to describe it, how it ended up that way. Not only did they get the shares and get the IP, but they also got our $50,000.

And then we arrived back at our desks to the Wells Notice from the SEC.

The original notification had said "in 10 days," and we had wondered whether they might have been hesitant to pull the trigger, because it seemed like a bit of a witch hunt, or based very thin ground. Seemingly not. They had gone from an informal investigation to a hearing, to a formal investigation, to a full Wells Notice, and we were now about to be sued.

In one way, it couldn't have come at a worse time. Because it rolled in just as I was preparing to travel to Ireland for our traditional family wedding, with all our friends and family around for the celebration.

5: Settlements and Honeymoons

As time went on, I had become comfortable with the fact that the SEC was a civil agency, meaning there was no threat of prison time or anything like that. But that's not what my initial feeling on it was. You just go to weird places in your head. I was thinking that maybe my business days in America were over.

I felt I'd been unlucky with it all. Joe D was in regular contact with me, saying he was working on several different angles, but I had to focus on Heidi and the family. The wedding was scheduled for September 7th 2018.

Joe was working away on the fact that, since the shares had never traded, there was never anyone harmed, and if he could push this line, they might be reasonable with us. I was beginning to get a sense that we were going into the SEC in a very different way. We had money to defend ourselves, we had a hot-shot New York attorney and it was now a different story. It seemed like they were starting to be willing to talk, whereas before it was just a cold, *you guys are done*, sort of approach.

In the Wells Notice and the correspondence at the time, they said they were going to sue for a director ban for life. I would never be able trade a stock under $5 again, I would never be allowed to be an executive in a public company, and I would have to pay a fine of $100,000 – a hundred times more than I had at the time.

On one call we had with Joe I actually said, "This is Bernie Madoff stuff here, Joe, this is outlandish, what are they trying to do? Surely there's a conversation to be had for a settlement?" Joe responded, "This IS the settlement offer." He was almost as bewildered as I was.

There are people who have run Ponzi schemes who have settled for fractions of that amount. I was just baffled, and thinking that maybe it was some kind of a sign. Maybe I should not be doing work or business in America. Maybe I need to just move home to Ireland and be done with it.

But I had to try to forget about it all for a while and get married. In the end we had an incredible day with our friends and families in Palmerstown House Hotel in Kildare and went off on the honeymoon. Heidi had been through all of this nightmare with me. She was a big part of the emotion of it all, and we had to agree to not think about things, to just go and have fun.

We had saved hard for a honeymoon and wanted to enjoy it. We went to Nice first in the South of France, and then we did a very unplanned tour of Italy. Remember that investor who put the first $100k into the company back in 2016? He sent us a wedding gift of a fully-paid vacation in Italy, to add on to the honeymoon. It was brilliant, I mean thanks so much! This investor went as far as to set us up in a vineyard for a couple of nights owned by a friend of his, who today, interestingly, is now a shareholder. It is funny how those things play out.

1. First award: South Dublin IBYE (Ireland's Best Young Entrepreneur) winner and cheque for €20,000

2. Signing my name – and officially opening trading on Wall Street – at our bell ceremony, December 3 2021

3. On our impromptu move to Ohio: one of many U-Haul trips across the USA in Heidi's 20-year-old Lexus banger

4. Speaking on the importance of AVERSA prior to opening the market at the NASDAQ bell ceremony, 3 December 2021

5. Heidi and I repping each other's jerseys, one of our earlier pics together

6. Team Sheridan

7. Taking Róe to see the blossoms in Salt Lake City while my parents are visiting, April 2023

8. At the Orlando Magic with my brother, Aáron

9. Following the Opening Bell Ceremony, Times Square, December 3 2021, with Dad, Mum, me, Heidi, Ned and Kathy (Heidi's Parents)

0. Kathy, Geri, Gareth, Heidi, Roy, Ned – on our Wedding Day

11. Aáron, Emily, Dad, Mum, Gareth, Heidi – Quito, Ecuador –
at Serguei and Jazmina's vow renewal - Dec 2021

12. The men! Top left to bottom right: Johnny, Simey, Gareth, Jeff,
Boland, Maughan, Gilly, McGlynn, Rougles, Jennings, Digo,
McSharry, Foxy, Chopper (Lukey honorably missing)

13. With Serguei after signing our first partnership with the Orlando Magic basketball team

14. Taking Serguei to his first rugby match: Ireland v France at the AVIVA

15. Heidi, Róe and Gareth - outside our Salt Lake house

16. 09:30 am, Dec 3 2021: The market is open for trading

I remember on one of the nights he organised a multiple-course dinner, sampling of the house wines etc, and went as far as to call the restaurant to speak to us and wish us well. I thought it was a very nice touch. We were most definitely getting a taste of how things could look like if we were to succeed in building Nutriband as planned.

On our second night in Italy, I got a call from Joe who said, "Great news, the SEC have just told me that they're willing to settle. We're going through the ins and outs of it now, but it's going to be a no-admit, no-deny cease and desist settlement. There will be a monetary fine, much smaller than what was originally discussed, with no director bans or restrictions of anything else tied to you. You must agree to never make a mistake like that again and follow the instructions of the cease and desist. You also cannot deny that you were in the wrong, but you do not have to admit you were either. So if anyone from the SEC is reading this book, I do not deny that we made errors in our judgement and I do not deny that we were wrong. But I also do not admit we were wrong. Anyway moving on ...

Joe D is a really good attorney, I've nothing but respect for him. He did a cracking job. He is at the top of my list of people I have ever worked with, because he saved everything essentially. When we rang the bell at NASDAQ, he was one of the first people I called to say, "You make sure you're there at the ceremony!"

Imagine hearing you have to pay a fine, and it's the best news ever! I honestly didn't care if it was all the money in the world, as long as I was not going to be blacklisted and kicked out of my own company, and I was not going to have that against my name. Joe said we'd have everything confirmed in the following week or two, but that "This is as good an outcome as we could have expected, congratulations!"

Heidi could see it on my face. We were sitting in the Airbnb in Italy at the time and she could see the dread draining from my face. It was such a load off, and for it to happen on our honeymoon was just perfect. I barely got the words out that the SEC are ready to settle, before she gave an enormous cheer and grabbed a bottle of wine, and the rest of the honeymoon was just fantastic.

Then, when we got back to Dublin, I got another phone call from Joe with the details and I thought, here we go, here's the moment of truth. The SEC wanted a $25,000 fine from each of us, which had to come from a personal account, not paid for by the company. I knew I didn't have that, but I'd figure it out.

Interestingly, the SEC wanted Serguei's $25,000 up front immediately, but they were willing to let mine come in instalments. I put that down to the fact that Serguei went in yelling, and the guys just wanted to slap him back a bit.

The same investor who paid for the Italian part of our honeymoon loaned my $25,000 as well, and I told him I would pay it back to him as soon as possible, and that I was going to make sure that he'd do well on his shares too. He told me he had every faith in that. "Just get it done," he said, "And put it behind you."

Last year I was in the nice position where I was able to pay him back in full. I told him I would make sure he sees a big return on his shares. That was a great feeling.

The censure from the SEC in the end was a slap on the wrist, a warning to make sure that in future all the i's are dotted and the t's are crossed. Had it been anything more than that, we probably wouldn't be listed today. So it was a pivotal moment in our story.

By then we were heading into 2019 thinking, 'This is our year, the year that we get our NASDAQ listing,' and the year we'd start fulfilling all of this.

While we lived in Ohio, despite the fact that we were caught up in lawsuits during those years, we still managed to move forward, one achievement being to acquire a company called 4P Therapeutics out of Atlanta which we had ultimately completed in August 2018. It was a company that we had been aware of, and so at one point I sat down with them to see if the owners of the company were interested in what we're doing. I approached it as if they might be the next piece of the jigsaw.

It was a long shot that they would talk to us, but we felt that out of all the current technology companies that we knew of, these guys were the real deal. They had their PhDs, they knew what they were at, there was no messing there. They'd been around, they were generating revenues, they came from backgrounds like Altea Therapeutics or Kimberly Clark – the latter being worth about $50 Billion today.

I said, "I can see from your financials, and from what you are doing with Defent (a product which was later further developed into our AVERSA technology), that everything is going great for you guys, but I think it would look much better as part of what we are building with Nutriband, and I think 4P could be a cornerstone of the company if we talked it through."

The owner of the company, Steve Damon, said they were looking at options on financing, etc. I explained what we were working on and pointed out that if they could believe in what we're trying to do, this would be a really good addition. And Steve said, "You know, to be honest, I believe that you can do it."

In our conversation, he mentioned how he wasn't getting any younger, and maybe didn't have as much energy as before. Then he said something that I'll always remember. He said, "I really like everything you said, and I like you as a person. I think if anybody's going to take this on, well – you're the guy to do it."

I was so delighted with his trust. This was the one technology that I'd seen since I'd moved to America that I was really excited about, that I thought could be a game changer. And so we signed the acquisition with 4P Therapeutics in April of 2018.

The deal was worth $1.9 Million, made up of 250,000 shares and $400,000 cash. Steve also received a board seat and was able to provide excellent guidance and experience for the next few years. Had we not received the big Irish investment, we wouldn't have had the $400,000 to acquire them, so we did the deal based on that investment.

That was something really big. Now we actually had a facility, we had equipment, we were able to do clinical trials. This was a big move for the company, a huge jump. While Steve eventually moved on from the board and picked up a CEO position with a microneedle company, he remained as an advisor. It was a great partnership for us.

Meanwhile, I was still working away with the banks and completing the relevant filings that we needed for our NASDAQ application. We eventually filed our NASDAQ application in early 2019. So in the space of only six months I'd been involved in multiple lawsuits and experienced the possibly of being removed as a director from my own company, and I remember just looking at the application going into NASDAQ and thinking, "This is it now, we've been through the worst."

But despite the silver lining, the hard work and anticipation, we were still actually only halfway through, and there were many more hurdles ahead. When the NASDAQ application went in, I called our attorney to ask how long it would take. He said that NASDAQ had been having some backlogs recently, so it would probably take month or two.

Given everything we'd been through, I could live with that. I thought we'd just keep working on the business, we'd keep generating revenue with 4P, and we'd wait and see what happens on the appeal with Advanced, to see if we can get the shares back for the company.

But in March 2020, after months of back and forth, NASDAQ came back and essentially said they didn't like the fact that not so long ago, we'd had a run in with the SEC, so we were rejected. How this works, typically, is that you can either appeal your rejection (but in doing so you must publicly file that NASDAQ rejected your application), or you can withdraw your application, take their advice and guidelines on board, and try again at later point in time. So because of our SEC issue, NASDAQ thought we were not well-enough set up for them, they thought we were not quite ready, and they wanted us to go away and work on the company for a year, and to try again. So that's what we had to do.

I would say the phone call from our attorney to give me the news was one of the worst phone calls I have ever received. Here we are, having fought through so much to get to this point, to fulfil the plan we started in January of 2016, only to get denied right at the finish line – not by a regulator, not by a bad acquisition, but by the NASDAQ itself.

We had our first rejection, but we could regroup, we could take on board all that was said and start again. Which would have been all very well if Covid hadn't hit, with government shutdowns and all sorts of other issues! We could do nothing but keep working on the business and try to make sure our application was absolutely amazing for when we re-filed again. We wanted things to be perfect.

As a result of our acquisition strategy that year, we grew the company from having $700,000 in shareholder equity and no assets to having $7.5 million in shareholder equity and $10 million in assets. When we resubmitted our NASDAQ application one year later, the analyst and NASDAQ looked at it and said, "This is great, we like what you guys have been able to do." Our analyst was just about to start working on the file. ... And then our analyst left NASDAQ! But I will come back to that.

It was March 2021 when we re-filed again, almost one year to the day after we had withdrawn our initial application. By then we had made another big acquisition, Pocono Pharmaceutical, which is the manufacturing facility we now own. In that case we had met with them, we sat down, we talked about our strategic plans, and outlined how we had successfully brought 4P Therapeutics in.

I sold it in a way that said, "All we're missing now is the capability to make our own products. We can design our own products, we can do clinical research – imagine if we could make our own products. This is where you guys fit the picture now." And they came on board. They were generating a revenue of a couple of million a year at this point, and they were an expensive acquisition for us. They cost $600,000 in cash and $6.9 million in stock. But they leapfrogged our equity into a position where we were more than qualified for our NASDAQ re-application.

Of course there were the ones that got away too. Before Pocono, we were in talks with an Australian company called New Medico. They had supposedly designed a safety technology for injections, in line what we were doing on the safety side. It was before we had accepted the first NASDAQ denial and had withdrawn the application. We thought that if we could get our shareholder equity up really quickly, and make a stronger case, NASDAQ would forget about the former SEC issue. I started looking at New Medico more closely, and I asked them to send me their financials, their revenues, their projections.

They sent projected revenues for 2020 of $40 million. My question to them was, how were they going to go from zero to forty? The CEO said that they had a number of purchase orders, because they had just made an agreement with the government of the Philippines. So we talked some more, and he told me he was still interested in the deal, but that he had board members and other people he had to run it by.

We quickly scrambled to make the deal happen, and we had signed off on everything – yet on the day of finalising the deal, when I called him he didn't answer. I messaged to say we'd sent over the paperwork, that today was the closing day, everything was lined up, NASDAQ were waiting to see the outcome of this, and "what's going on?" And he messaged back saying, "I'll have to get back to you."

At that point, there were only a couple of hours left in the day, we had a deal to do, and he was just ghosting me. Eventually I got a cryptic message saying, "Sorry, one board member didn't want to do it, and you know – good luck."

I did not know what had just happened. The guy went from being a friendly, nice, pleasant person to just cutting us off, black and white. I felt like we had been played. Apparently, they got the notion that they could do it better by themselves, without us, but actually that company never went anywhere in the end. I often wonder if they were using us to try get a better deal elsewhere or what exactly their angle was.

When we eventually listed on NASDAQ, he sent me a message saying, "Congratulations – and let me know when you're free to catch up!" And I thought, "You'll be waiting by the phone for a while, pal ..." It was a disappointing moment, yet again, and the last gasp attempt to save that particular NASDAQ filing.

Our second application for the NASDAQ was also complicated. If you remember, following our withdrawal the first time, an analyst who told us he was on our case just suddenly left. After that we were passed on to another NASDAQ analyst, who confirmed that she had subsequently picked up the file. But she basically denied us again for the exact same reasons we were penalised for the first time, the former SEC issue. And again – she said she didn't feel we were quite ready. It was like a double jeopardy. We had been told to serve our time, bolster up the value in the company and come back well behaved – and we did just that, and we got a second denial for the same reason.

It was the most stressful period of my life, bar none. It was a feeling like I've never had before or since, or could probably even describe. I remember exactly where I was, exactly what was going on. Just when I thought we were through the worst of it, it came as a killer blow.

At the time of the first rejection we got from NASDAQ, I was worth millions of dollars on paper. We were still over the counter at the time, so we didn't put much emphasis on value, but if anybody else were to look at it, it looked great. In reality, the day we got our first denial I was sitting in a Hertz car park, waiting to pick up a car to go to work driving for Uber at $6.50 an hour because our car didn't meet the safety standards to be a driver ...

The second one was so much harder, because we thought by then we were well on the way, that we were entering the big league, we had done everything that was asked of us and then some, and yet we were told again we couldn't join the club.

We had to hire a specialist, an ex-NASDAQ listing analyst this time, and we had to pay them $50,000 to fight our case. Coincidently this specialist had actually been an associate on our first listing application which was denied, it was only years later when looking back at some correspondence I noticed her name cc'd in the emails. Anyway, It added another seven months to the process. Around September of 2021, it went all the way up to some superiors at NASDAQ, who overturned the second rejection and gave us the go ahead.

I was having lunch with Heidi in Panama City Beach in Florida where Heidi was working on an interior design project and I had flown in just to spend a few days with her. We were in a Crab Shack on the beach and the email came in, and I said, "You are not going to believe this, we just got the green light to list." We were both really quiet for a few seconds and I said, "I need to make sure this isn't a hoax." It had just taken so long to get to that point.

The email was from the consultant who had been working on it with us, and in it she said, "We're going to have to prepare all the final bits and pieces they want, but it looks like they're not going to enforce the second rejection, so let's get to work – let's get all the material in."

We finished up our lunch pretty quickly, and went straight back to the house that Heidi was working in, where we were staying. What Heidi used to do in those days, to support the big dream, was to sleep in the house where she was working, instead of a hotel, to save money. I only learned later that one of the houses she was working in was in a dodgy area, there was no front door on the house, and she went right ahead and slept in it. That's her personality, to get on with things. Mind you, her dad Ned wasn't very happy when he found out about it.

But that day, luckily, the Wi-Fi in the house was still connected during the renovations, so I got to work on the NASDAQ stuff, and there was what I can only describe as a kind of dreamlike ease in the air. So much pressure and negativity had been lifted, even if I didn't quite believe it was true just yet. We were just kind of floating, it was the polar opposite of the feeling when we received our first rejection, it's how I imagine it must be if you were suddenly told you'd won the Lotto, very hard to describe.

A few days later all the paperwork was in, and we got a notification, almost casually, that they wanted us to list us in the morning. The whole tone of everything had changed. It was not *explain yourself* emails any more, just process stuff, minor details, almost boring.

Were we over the line then? Not quite! We were good to go, we had our listing date, and then the night before we were supposed to list, our auditors or someone involved in the process, didn't return a phone call, or something was missing from the file, and we had to call the NASDAQ back and say, "uh, we're actually not quite ready ..." A bit embarrassing, not the most ideal situation, but in the end it just pushed things out by another day.

Finally, after all the hard work and two rejections, we were on the cusp of joining the exclusive club. Serguei and I always say now that those things happen so that you fully appreciate achievement when it does come along. If it all was easy, and it came to us quickly, we probably wouldn't have managed the company as well. Maybe we would have been those million-dollar salary guys who destroy their companies.

Ninety per cent of biotech companies in our space and our size fail, because they go back to the market, raise money, raise money, raise money, and they are doing it at a lower valuation every time. Before they know it, the banks are in the boardroom and the CEOs are fired, and the bank strips it for parts and sells it at rock bottom. Serguei has a simple response these days for people that ask us about investing or raising capital for us, which I have also adopted. We just say that we are not in the business of *raising money*.

It's something I had to learn, because I remember when we were really short on capital in the earlier days, somebody offered us a million dollars. And I thought, wow, a million dollars – we were going to be able to do so much with this. It was actually Serguei that said that we couldn't take it, because down the line in a few years' time, that million dollars would really come back and bite us in the backside, because the terms were convertible.

This means that when they give you your $1m, you might be up at $4 a share. Then that person who loaned it or who invested starts shorting your stock down to 20 cents. They convert their $1m at 20 cents and all of a sudden, their equity is far higher than you thought you were giving away for the $1m. It happens all the time. So turning that down was a first, but turning money down later, since then, has become very easy. The first million dollars is a very difficult thing to turn down.

I think the other flaw I have seen is that is that when companies list on the NASDAQ, they have no revenues. They are three years out from filing for approval for the product with the FDA. They raise $10 million, and all of a sudden, all the executives are paying themselves a million a year, and they are burning through the money.

We pay ourselves in the bottom 10% of NASDAQ companies, because if we were a private company, that's how it would be, how we would act, and how we would be performing. The value in the share is long term, not to make a million dollars quickly. The value is to make many millions of dollars in a few years.

Many companies and CEOs and executives, I feel, take the other pathway. They make their million-dollar salary for maybe two years, but then they are out of the company, the company is struggling – it's completely down – stock value is gone, and it is all over. Quite a few companies that listed five places before us or five after us in this field are now under a dollar a share.

Our plan was always to buy a company or companies that make about two or three million dollars a year, and to have that company pay all of the overheads, so that the invested money, from earlier on, which we still have now by the way, would be put into the FDA process. So there's no cross over, there's no stupid spend. You run things efficiently and that will eventually pay off in a much bigger way than having a big salary for two years, and then having your company struggle, getting squeezed out, or getting sued by your shareholders.

Our approach has resonated with a lot of people. I paid myself a $5,000 bonus last year. Most bonuses for a CEO of a NASDAQ company are hundreds of thousands for the year. I was presenting to a fund recently and they asked what my bonus was last year, what the executive compensation was. And I replied "Five". He thought I meant $500,000. And I said, "No, $5,000. There was silence for a moment, and he says, "Oh, I see ... that's unheard of. But I like you guys' style."

But the goal here is to have a stock that's going to be vastly better valued than those around us who are getting into mad spending. And that comes back again to choosing the right partners, something I think you learn as you go. I've gotten it to a point where there are certain mannerisms that I can't stand in people, things that are a complete red flag, like if they click at a waiter in a restaurant, for example, you know they're going to be a problem.

I was lucky that I connected with Serguei when I did, and I'd say I learned a lot from him in terms of picking my partners, because up till then he had done nothing but pick wrong partners. We would talk about it, and discuss what to look for, what to take seriously, and what to not take seriously.

At this stage I could have a PhD in classifying people as difficult, or just not right for now. But you can only learn through making mistakes, you have to experience it. It's not something you can learn from a book. You have to have had issues picking wrong partners to know how to not pick them again, and you have to understand when you have a good partner not to let them go, or not to damage that relationship. People will sometimes act like your best friend and say they want nothing but the best for you, and it is not the case at all.

I remember there was an independent board member at one time – who had been brought on to the board by Serguei. He called me up one day to say that he thought Serguei was kind of hot-headed, how we needed to be careful how this could impact the company. We needed to be really careful going forward that he was not responsible for managing certain things ... And I thought, this guy's trying to build himself into a bigger position. My loyalty was obviously going to be with Serguei, so I spoke to him and we straight away made the necessary moves to get him off the board. And that was it! We had no issues with him, but he would definitely have been a problem. He's actually a nice guy, and Serguei still goes to games with him when we're in New York, and they'll hang out together. I don't think I ever even mentioned to Serguei that he talked that way, just that he was not a fit for us.

Another time he'd said something along the lines of how we needed to settle the Advanced Health lawsuit. He figured we should just give them what they wanted and move on from it. And I thought, it's too easy for him to say that when he doesn't even know what's going on! I knew he just didn't want it connected to his name. And you know, if you're afraid of a lawsuit, then maybe you shouldn't be on a board. If you want to be part of a NASDAQ company and you want to make a difference, you can't be afraid of a professional argument, which is all a lawsuit really is.

After our listing in October of 2021 and into 2022, the appeal against Advanced Health was underway and, as predicted, it was taking its own good time. But we had work to do and a business to grow, dealing with all the Covid lockdowns and the extra slow bureaucratic process with applications.

Then we had a flurry of patent approvals for our patch technology and that led to more interest in us. Such as interest from Kindeva – formerly known as 3M Drug Delivery – which became the start of another great relationship for us. Way back in 2014, in the very early days of Nutriband, I had reached out to 3M to see if we could work together on some of the formulations. I'd thought they could manufacture some of the products that I was looking at, but they had shrugged me off. And rightfully so when I think back now, since I had no business working with a company that big for my vitamin patches. My feeling at the time was that they were thinking, "We're too big for you, we don't deal with people like you," that kind of thing, and I was naively offended almost. Silly really, when I think back.

Then within a week of our NASDAQ listing, we're all best friends. The same core team want to work with me. It was quite interesting to finally get acknowledgment from a company you want to work with, albeit years after the initial reach-out. Things like that stay with you. You can believe in your idea all you want, but it becomes real when people around you start to believe it too.

It all started to come together for us. We got the first US patent a couple of days before we finally got confirmation of our NASDAQ listing, and then we signed an agreement with Kindeva all in a very short space of time. It was like the stars aligned a little bit out there.

Suddenly, I found I was a NASDAQ CEO – and then all kinds of people are happy to take your calls, and are calling you, the very people who had no interest in talking to you before. We had been working intently on our AVERSA product at this time, and developing it with the resources we had, filing patent applications, reaching out to companies, etc, but nothing was sticking. Then we got the NASDAQ notification and we were having partnership discussions with the best.

Kindeva drug delivery is one of the biggest Transdermal Pharma manufacturers globally, one of two that basically own the transdermal space – the other is LTS Lohmann in Germany. By then we had been issued our US patent, so Kindeva took a keen interest in working with us to co-develop AVERSA Fentanyl, the first AVERSA product. Kindeva already makes generic fentanyl patches, our strategy was to use our IP and add our AVERSA tech to their approved generic and relaunch the new and improved AVERSA Fentanyl patch for chronic pain and we are on track to do that today. We have very strong relationship now and I imagine we will develop more AVERSA products together in the coming years.

There are other products out there in the pain management space which use patch technology, and claim they work well, but which I am convinced actually don't work at all. One product that's interestingly approved by the FDA for decades now, is a lidocaine patch and it's used to treat moderate pain. All the science says that there's no way it should work, and yet people get significant relief from it. So that's an anomaly in the direct space in which we are working.

All of the basic science would say that a lidocaine patch should not work as it does, but all of the data would say different – it's quite fascinating actually.

So you could say that's a sub-group in the space that is still being discovered. On the other hand, pain is subjective and if enough people say that something works, then it snowballs and people believe it works. It's a tricky one.

What we have patented is the use of aversive agents, very nasty ingredients on the back of an existing patch that make it almost impossible to chew, smoke, or swallow to get a high from the contents of the patch. That's what our patent is based on, and it is a platform technology that can be added to any patch on the market today.

A typical fentanyl pain management patch on the market today is basically a three-layer patch. Over a base liner you have a drug layer, and then you have a backing layer, which is a bit like a band aid. It's worn like that. But residual fentanyl inside the patch can remain, even after use, in high quantities. You can have up to 70% residual fentanyl left in that patch in many circumstances.

If you imagine that fentanyl can be fifty times stronger than heroin, you can see how appealing it is for someone with addiction or looking to get a high to chew one of those patches, like chewing tobacco, or to try to smoke the contents, or use it like a tea bag. It is wide open to abuse. What our tech does is to mix any residual fentanyl with two ingredients we put on the back of the patch, which makes it really, really unpleasant – in fact, dreadful – if someone were to try and misuse it. So if a person tries to smoke it or chew it or anything else, the experience for that individual will be "unbearable" – this being the most suitable word, I think, to describe it. I've tried it personally, to have the experience, not with fentanyl or any other drug in the patch, just to see what the ingredients were like, and believe me it's something I won't forget. The goal ultimately is to make misusing these patches – whether accidentally or purposefully – extremely disgusting to the senses. On the plus side however, if you use them correctly, you would not even know that the ingredients were there, that is the beauty of AVERSA.

AVERSA patches work exactly like the other patches on the market today that we are trying to replace, in fact they are scientifically identical to the generics in terms of the relief profile because they are exactly those patches just adding a new external layer, AVERSA.

But the problem with most transdermal patches is that they can be deliberately abused – or even inadvertently misused. There are documented cases of children who have picked a patch out of a bin, put it in their mouths, and the residual fentanyl has killed them. The Poison Control Centre in the States has at least five reported deaths of children under the age of five who did this in recent years, as an actual data point that is being monitored by The Poison Control Centre, not just a once-off incident, but now something that has developed a category of its own which is under watch. Little hands who innocently pick up a patch with no built in safety mechanism, that was discarded without thinking. There have been dozens more hospitalisations on top of that again. Deaths that are so avoidable and tragic.

Fentanyl is an extremely potent drug. To give you an idea, when there are reports of a fentanyl overdose in America, the first responders in many cases show up in a hazmat suit. This is because there could be enough fentanyl left in the air to kill or seriously harm them, or at the least, cause an overdose. There are also videos on YouTube of police officers pulling someone over and searching their car only to come across a bag of fentanyl, open it and go straight into an overdose state from the amount that was released into the air. Many police officers now carry Narcan with them for these reasons. Narcan counters the effects of opioid overdose.

I always wanted to use transdermal tech to improve outcomes for patients with severe pain – not that we set out to be a socially responsible, do-gooder kind of company in the first instance – but I would say we have definitely leaned into that role.

We knew we could sell this product probably for many multiples of dollars of what we're planning to sell it for, and shareholders would be happy, but as I mentioned before, it's the rate of coverage for patients that we are really interested in. We can corner and take over this space entirely in my opinion at the expense of our competitors, not at the expense of the patients.

I have my own experience with this. My dad broke his back about seven years ago during the "Beast From The East" snowstorm. He was getting out of the car and just slipped on a mound of snow and fell straight down on his back. He was able to get up and walk initially, but then the next morning he couldn't move, and an ambulance was called. He had fractured two of his vertebrae, which he's never really recovered from. He's tried patches, he's tried all the treatments, but he can hardly walk from A to B and he's pushing 80 this year. And you know, there's a reluctance for prescribers in Ireland to give him the type of treatments that I would like to see him get.

It's funny how it worked out that way, because we had started working on this tech with AVERSA prior to that happening, but then living it first hand with a direct family member brought it home to me how important this work is.

Dad was trialled with a buprenorphine patch, which is a lesser strength opioid, something we are working on as well, but because he was already on certain other medications, they were reluctant to continue it. Of course whenever I ask him how his back is, in typical stubborn Irish fashion he'll just say, 'it's grand'.

I think they only prescribed it in the first instance because we all kicked up bit about his lack of access to adequate pain management, but there was no effort to maintain treatment, and I think that's the case right across the board, because there's currently too much risk. Prescribers are afraid to be associated with these products in the current state. I believe our technology will mitigate against that completely.

6: AVERSA and The Pain Crisis

I've been told numerous times that I must be very good at selling, and it's something I'm still trying to figure out. Is it a characteristic I have? Because it's not something that I would have ever thought of when describing myself. I think I'd be a terrible door-to-door salesman.

Maybe it started from around the time of the awards, when I was knocking my head against a wall trying to sell my idea to reluctant customers, and it just built and grew from there. But there was no defining moment where I thought, "this is what I do, I sell things, or persuade people." But definitely as you build your credibility, the doors start to open.

And then of course there is just shameless trying it on, reaching out to people, using LinkedIn, messaging people, doing your research, working through the list, that approach. Sometimes along the way, people were almost caught off guard by the directness of it. You try to sound credible and make it a no BS situation. It's direct and straightforward and you get to the point – there's no games.

But I did always reach out for an introduction feeling as if I were worthy of that introduction, that the idea merited an introduction, and that the difference we could make merited a hearing. Now I have weekly conversations with people who wouldn't answer the phone to me only three or four years ago.

I suppose there's a part of me that feels I should have been responded to, all along, the way I get responded to now. At the time, the closed doors and the meeting refusals didn't feel good. But I just decided that I'd add that person to the list of people to get back in touch with when it all worked out. You have to execute. If you tell people you're going to do something, then you had better do it.

One thing I sell now, if we want to use that word, is that everything that I have ever said we were going to do with the business, we have done. So, if you're concerned that I want to have a conversation with you in this coming year, just look at our last five years and you will see that everything we told you was going to happen, has happened.

When I give talks to colleges or start-up groups, I always say the main thing is not to take the refusals personally. I'm a fine one to talk, because I took it all very personally at the start. But I think I quickly grew out of that during the investment years and learned not to take the word no as a deterrent.

Don't get down about things. If you reach out to somebody and they don't respond, it could be that it is just not the right time. It doesn't mean that it won't be the right time later, as you continue to prove yourself. When I look back, that was the thing, I was constantly trying to prove myself, a complete greenhorn, to a very established group of businesses and people.

Now I think we've a good reputation as a company. But we were nobodies back then, even though we might have thought differently. It is just something you have to go through, like a football team coming up the ranks in different leagues. You eventually get to the Premier League, and everybody goes to your matches, but nobody cares about you when you're in league five, even if you think you deserve to be in league one.

Nowadays I always try to be accessible, to take those calls, because of how it didn't feel good when I was on the other side. But I understand why it happened. I get a lot of calls from younger Irish entrepreneurs, particularly in the health field, who reach out and ask for advice. There is one guy in particular, Alex, who's moved to San Francisco with a very interesting medical device company, who is doing some fundraising. He asked me for advice on how the product would be classified with the FDA, and I'm happy to at least try give him a steer or connect him to the right person.

Every now and then I'll miss a text or a WhatsApp message from someone, but it's not on purpose. It could be just scheduling issues. I'll feel bad about it, and I try to reach back out when I can get to it. It might take three days to respond, but I'll never leave someone hanging if I can. I remember being in that position, and being on the other side of it, so I definitely don't want to be the one inflicting it.

Another thing I am selling these days is the value of opioids in pain management. You have to look at it logically. Nobody can justify what the likes of Purdue and similar companies did in causing addiction, but the reality is that there is no suitable replacement to opioid treatment on the market today. There is nothing of proof that is comparable, and you have to take into consideration that broader group – the whole pain community and patient group – that don't have access to adequate treatments now because of the negative stigma caused by those bad actors.

Prescription rates in opioids have plummeted because there's a reluctance and a negative stigma associated with these drugs now, and nobody wants the fallback. Doctors don't want to take the risk of prescribing them because of the potential liability. That has a huge knock-on effect, because you have an increasing patient group that can't get access to the treatment. And when people can't get prescriptions from the doctor, what do they do? They buy the illegal fentanyl, the illegal opioids, and that just snowballs the issue.

Suicide rates in the pain population have gone up drastically because of inadequate treatment levels. So it's a far more complicated issue than people give credit to. When used correctly, opioids are second to none for adequate pain management. So you have to find a happy medium.

While everybody else was rushing away from the space fearfully, we looked at that as an opportunity to come in and become the market leader. And that's the solution we worked on. Because the pain population is equally as important as the addiction population – and they've been overlooked for almost ten years now.

The reality is that fentanyl should be used for spinal injuries, palliative care, serious issues. Usually when somebody is going on fentanyl, they're not coming off it again. It's to make them comfortable. The problem is that companies like Insys or the Sackler family were pushing doctors to prescribe fentanyl and opiates for a toothache, or a headache. Somebody gets a crown on their tooth and all of a sudden, they've got a 30-day supply of Oxycontin. It was appalling carry on. And it ruined what was a promising treatment space for pain.

The end result was that you had people with major injuries suddenly denied access to opioids – told to go home and take Panadol or Ibuprofen. I mean there's no way at all that somebody who is reliant on opioids for treating pain should be given something that's suitable for an eight-year-old with a fever. That's the disconnect, and because of the lawsuits involved, because of the name *opioid* even, everybody shied away from it and just ignored it.

The illegal market is now flourishing, because you only need a tiny amount to get high. It's very easy to import illegally. Instead of bringing a shipping container of cocaine or heroin, criminals can import just a backpack of fentanyl and get the same results. So there are a lot of logistical benefits for the criminal world, which is creating a huge issue.

In addition, you have other drugs that are being laced with fentanyl to increase the high, and it is incredible how many people are impacted. I heard of a case where a guy I knew in my school years., went to Miami on a stag weekend, and decided for whatever reason to do cocaine. It was laced with fentanyl, and he unfortunately overdosed and died. I think he was early thirties when it happened. He had a twin, and a family at home in Ireland. You don't think about something like that when you go on a stag weekend.

It's a major, major problem. I know we're not going to solve the fentanyl issues – there's always going to be illegal fentanyl, there are always going to be illegal opioids. But I think we can make a very big dent in the abuse of prescription opioids. I mentioned to Serguei recently that yet another person had approached me after a talk I had given, to say their son had died from an overdose, and Serguei came back with yet another tragic story.

The father of one of his own close friends, who had a spinal injury, and who couldn't get adequate treatment, had just taken his own life. He left a note behind saying he was so sorry, he didn't want to go, but he just couldn't bear the pain anymore. That's another terrible element of the mess in the opioid space – the suicide rates. Efficient pain management is just completely mismanaged from start to finish, because of all the bad actors who have ruined it for multiple groups.

We're in a very small niche that can do very well as a company and also do very well in terms of making a difference for humanity. Yet if you want to continue to add new products and new technology, you have to make money as a company, that's how the world works.

But we are never going to jump into the big pharma mentality that is despised by so many. We want to actually try to put manners on those guys. We're coming into a place where the big companies are still selling the generic patches, turning a blind eye to the kids pulling them out of dumpsters. We want to take the whole market out from under them, to provide safe pain management patches. We want to lock in a price that's going to be affordable, and make sure people worldwide have access to essential treatments. Nothing is 100% safe, we know that. But our product is 99% safer than anything else out there at the moment, and I stand by that.

So we are and will continue to be a patient-focused pharma company, and that's something that's pretty rare in the Pharma world. I remember talking some of this through with Steve Damon, the then CEO of 4P Therapeutics, and Alan Smith, who's still the lead scientist on our team, when we sat down with them first. They agreed that our approach was unprecedented, both in terms of our growth strategy and how we wanted to be disruptors, to be patient-focused in a way that currently doesn't really exist.

I mentioned that Steve has always been a supporter and has provided guidance. One thing that stands out from that meeting is when he asked, where do you want to go with this? And I told him straight away that we would be a billion-dollar company, we would get there, and that I thought we would get there within a specific timeframe.

I wrote it on a napkin in the 'Buffalo Wild Wings' restaurant where we were having dinner, and he has that napkin today in his briefcase! Every time I meet with him, he brings the napkin. In a way, it's important that he held onto it, and didn't throw it away, or ignore it. I mean, he believed it, and that was the big thing. We did tell him we were going to be NASDAQ-listed long before we actually got there, but he understood the delays and the rejections.

The early version of the tech 4P were working on at the time was called Defent, which we thought was an awful name, and we renamed the next generation version as AVERSA. That's the one we are working on now. I think we came in at a good time for everybody, with energy and enthusiasm, and we approached it in a new and different way. All the while, Alan Smith, our COO, is still at the helm of the project through the transition and has been instrumental in taking it from concept through to reality, which I'm sure it is a nice feeling for him too.

The AVERSA tech, or transdermal tech overall, is what we focus on. We are looking at buprenorphine too, a lesser strength opioid, which is in our pipeline. It's used to treat moderate to severe pain, as opposed to extreme severe pain. We are also developing an AVERSA version of methylphenidate which is an abusable ADHD medication. So the applications for AVERSA are very broad, which is part of its value.

In that regard, we're looking at buprenorphine through a different lens too, since it is chemically a suitable replacement for methadone. We're looking at the concept of introducing it into the methadone clinic system. With traditional methadone treatments, people usually get liquid methadone in a dose that may be taken over the course of a couple days. Instead, they could receive patches, where one patch could be designed to deliver the treatment over four days. Unlike methadone, however, the beauty of our idea is that it would not be easy to abuse, use incorrectly or even sell to someone with addiction, which are all issues that flaw the methadone clinic system today. Methadone in its current form can be abused and sold. To put it another way, think of a nicotine patch for opioid addiction, one that would be very difficult to abuse.

It expands beyond that again with lots of different technologies. We have a proprietary tech for delivering peptides which fall into the diabetes category, for patch delivery of exenatide, which is a type of diabetes medication similar to insulin. That one is a longer, more expensive one to develop, but if it's successful, we could cut out the use of needles for Type 2 diabetics. But that's a few years down the line yet and very early days.

7: Shark Fests and Naked Shorts

It's hard to believe, really, that we're where we are at today as a result of using our stock as an acquisition currency – in a strategy that we developed. And it worked out very well. Ninety-nine percent of the value of the company today was bought with about four percent in equity. So the strategy and the thesis behind it worked. That's something I talk about a lot with entrepreneurial students. I maintain that you have to aim to break the mould. You don't have to be a billion-dollar company to list, to become public, to take that journey. But this is not in the business books – you don't learn that in school. It was just a concept we had that we ran with, and it worked.

I don't know how many other companies have done it, and I realise that not everyone gets to the level of a NASADAQ listing. You might have companies that have done it, or tried it, where it has all just been a scheme and they've ended up costing people lots of money. But I don't think that taking a $100,000 investment and turning it into a hundred million dollars in nine years is a luck thing. It's what we have been able to achieve through our concept.

And no matter how negative this story is in places, it wasn't necessarily a playing field where I ever felt uncomfortable. Because you really appreciate the wins when they happen, and you really appreciate how much you have learned about people, and how they can behave.

There is a very nasty side to Wall Street. The shark-fest is built into the system, and I'm not just talking about pump and dump schemes in the mid-west or Florida. It's the mentality that is rampant, even among banks and institutions and among the trade publications. We've had hit pieces written about us by non-reputable websites, and we think there's possibly people involved in the sites that are trying to short us. For example, articles appeared that said the stock was about to go down to $1.50, or that I was grossly overpaid, when our pay structure is in the bottom ten percent of NASDAQ-listed companies.

When taking a short position, someone is betting that a stock is going to go down. The functionality of that is, they will borrow shares from somebody in the market. And there are systems and mechanisms already in place for that, going through your brokerage. Say the stock price is at $5, I'm betting that the stock price is probably going to go down to two or three dollars. How this works is I will borrow shares from you in the market and pay a borrow fee and sell them at the $5 price. When it does eventually go down, I'll buy the shares back in the market at $2/3 as I predicted, and give you back your shares. So I've made a couple of dollars on every share, you've got your shares back, along with whatever interest fee you charged me. Everybody happy, all going well.

Naked shorting is the same mechanism, except that the person selling the shares never borrows them in the first place. They are selling phantom shares. It's highly illegal, because it's manipulating the stock price, and that's a huge issue at the moment, which is not getting clamped down on from a regulatory standpoint, in my opinion.

There was one situation I heard of recently where naked shorting was carried out really aggressively by one particular 'investment bank', who made two million dollars in the transactions. They were caught, and the SEC and the regulators charged them, ultimately settling the case for $278,000. So they kept more than $1 million dollars. Reputationally, it didn't look good that the SEC put out an announcement on the case, but you know what, you can repair a reputation pretty quickly with the budgets they have and most funds will continue this shorting practice because they know they can get away with it by paying a fraction in penalties of what they gained. Ultimately the only loser is the company or shareholders in the company that they have targeted and damaged.

The system is broken because you can see there is no deterrent, people can make millions and millions of dollars, and then if they get caught, pay a fraction of that in a fine. It's built into the system, its built into the model. They are happy to create the fine. And yes, that's filthy.

The only way to protect yourself from the shorts is to execute on your plan, and raise as little money as possible along the way. Funds also heavily target companies they feel will continuously need to raise money because usually this is done at a discount to the trading price. So you will find situations where funds or individuals will short a stock at $3, the company announces a cash raise at $2 a share and the person or fund that has shorted can buy the shorted share back in the offering making a dollar profit.

You will even see situations where naked shorting is so aggressive that it drives prices down further and further inciting panic in genuine shareholders who then also jump ship and sell into the market as the pressure is too much. At this point they can cover their shares for a fraction of what they have been selling for as the stock has been sliding.

We work with a market maker now that gives us data on this, material we can use to challenge things with the regulators if we see dealing we don't think look right. We watch it very closely.

We recently came close to suing a publication in Australia because they put out a very negative hit piece on us. This was a mid-level outfit, not very reputable but at the same time you might have heard the name of the publication once or twice before. They've managed to wedge themselves into a place that is just above unreliable.

When I saw the article, I looked through it and literally checked off the facts, saying: "False, false, false, not true ..." None of what they were saying was true. But that article caused our stock to drop by $1.50 that day. We had to send them a threatening letter saying that we were preparing a legal action unless they recanted it and put out a fresh piece.

I reached out to the CEO of the publication on LinkedIn and went through him. I let him have it, because we had lost $15 million in value that day because of that one article! Then I started getting phone calls from shareholders, asking what this was about? I had to tell them it was a deliberate hit piece, that there was nothing valid in the article, that we were working on it.

They partly took back what they said, and we kept sending them legal letters, and then we were advised by our attorney that we could send as many letters as we wanted, or we could sue them, but they were in Australia, so nothing much was going to come from it. By the same token, we could throw tens of thousands of dollars at it and even if we got a judgment, they were *still* in Australia, and more or less out of reach. The best thing was to overpower the negative piece with positive news.

The stock recovered, but it took about three or four weeks to recover a day's worth of damage. Meaning they probably made their money on their short. They did the hit piece, they cover their short position, they've made $1.50 a share. And we're picking up the pieces, not them.

We brought up our frustrations with NASDAQ, who told us they would look into it. But what can you do? They targeted us that week, they'll move on to someone else the following week, short that company in turn, put out a hit piece and go on their merry way.

And it is not only dodgy publications that do this. It can be so-called reputable banks. We were looking at raising money one time with a top New York bank when we needed operational costs to go towards AVERSA. They had been introduced to us by a mutual connection and were supposedly "one of the few good banks left on Wall Street," with a reputation of being "real good guys and supportive of the companies they work with."

We had been reluctant historically to do a raise this way, because of potential game playing. We always raised with our existing shareholders or their associates – minus our NASDAQ IPO that is. So we told this bank we were open to doing a raise with them, but the last thing we wanted to do was sign a deal to raise money, and then see our stocks start to trickle down for the next couple of weeks while we finalised it.

Because that's exactly what some banks do. You'll sign a deal with them. They'll start shorting your stock, all of a sudden you're no longer at $4.00, you're at $2.00, and then they do the deal at $1.50, and end up with more equity.

We told these "good guys" straight up that if we became aware of any sort of game playing, anything we didn't like, we would pull out of the deal and move on. They said, "no problem, we don't do that".

So we went ahead and signed the deal, we filed our S-1 with the SEC, and you guessed it – surprise, surprise – the stock closed 10% down first thing! And then 10% down the next day. Then it's 10% percent down the following day, and we watched it trickle down every day to a point where we hit our lowest ever valuation, even on the OTC.

The stock got as low as $1.90, and I'd never seen our stock start with a "one" before. And when you're a one, you're in very dangerous place, because if you drop below one, you're in de-listing territory. But all we could do was to watch this playing out in front of our eyes, and we're saying *these flaming effers are messing with us, messing with the stock ...*

A day before the deal had to be priced, they called up and said, "Look, you know, the stock is at $1.90, so we're going to have to do the deal at something like $1 a share, or at $1.50." So we just said, no, that the deal was off. We pointed out that when we initially started talking to them, a very short time before that, we were listed at $4.00 a share. And yet now that we were about to actually do the deal, they wanted to do it at a $1.50? We reminded them that we said from the beginning we were never going to do it at a decreased value. It had never been an option.

Their response was, "Yeah, well, you know, the market is the way the market is, and the stock is down, and we can't do anything about that because people don't want to buy at a premium."

We told everyone the deal was off, that we were going to file the following morning to withdraw the offering statement with the SEC, and move on from there. They tried to persuade us for some time, but we stuck to our guns and just said no, we will never raise money at these levels. "Okay, sorry it couldn't work out," they said. "Let us know if you change your mind, blah, blah, blah." We hung up the phone and the stock jumped 30% after market that evening, starting immediately after the call.

In normal circumstances, where you have been considering a deal like this, you put out a release saying you are not doing a raise after all. And usually when you are not doing an offering anymore, the stock reacts positively, because there's no dilution. Serguei and I had a think about it and agreed not to put out the news until about 9 am. Everybody in the bank was going to think that we would put out this news at 7 am, that they'd be able to buy back, and it would look like a market reaction.

So we schedule news to go out at 9 am. Pre-market trading had opened at 7 am, and our stock rallied by another 30%. By the time we put out the news two hours later, the stock was up 65% from the previous night's phone call, at an unusually high volume.

And then we knew. I mean, why, without any other catalyst, without any other news, would the stock rally by 30% that morning? Serguei sent a very nasty email to the bank saying, "We know what you did." Serguei is emotional, as I have said before. So he'll send the *you're all just scumbags* kind of email. I'm more of the level-headed one, or so I am told. We have a good-cop-bad-cop thing going on. It works quite well, actually.

We called up NASDAQ to complain, and told them we were going to send them all of the material on this situation and that we thought they needed to look at it because it was rampant in Wall Street, particularly with micro caps and smaller cap companies, and that something needed to be done. Within ten minutes, NASDAQ responded to us and – without divulging anything that may be confidential – we were happy with the actions that were being taken.

Now, if all that happened within 10 minutes, they could clearly see stuff we couldn't see. They could actually see the trades, they could see who was buying, they obviously saw where it was coming from. It is not something they would disclose to us, but we're fairly confident that there were some repercussions.

The bank actually had the nerve to sue us for their lost fees because we pulled out of the deal at the last minute. So we countersued them then for the lost market cap, which was $20 million, and all of a sudden, they went very quiet. It's actually still an active filing with the court, but nobody's done anything on it, because if it pushes forward, it goes to discovery, and that's potentially a big problem for them in my opinion.

Funnily enough, I was at a conference in Atlantic City in January of 2024 where that bank also attended. I remember sitting down at my table and a few of them came over all friendly – giving it the, "How's it going man, we've been following the company, we should raise you guys some money and work together." I just looked at them ... I responded slowly, trying to figure out what the story was.

It turns out they were not even aware of the lawsuit because once I told them that it probably was not a runner because they actually *sued* us, they just bluffed, "Oh – we will get rid of that man – sorry, it must have been a mistake." or some weird excuse. Anyway, I left wondering whether they were all high or something after that interaction. But it was just another example of how you can't take all those games and lawsuits and Wall Street carry on personally. So much so that they thought I was going to get up and give them a high five and start planning our next demise, I mean raise with them.

I'm sure that other investment banks or funds we know well have probably shorted our stock, or at least the investors they have introduced have. But we will still have dinner together when we are in New York, and look each other in the eye, and play friends, feeling each other out subtly. When it comes to investment bankers or family office funds, often, at the end of the day, if our stock performs, we're going to screw them, if our stock doesn't perform, they're going to screw us, and it's a game we're all playing.

There are no personal feelings with it, and you have to learn to adapt to that mentality. You can go for dinner with a fund one night, and they'll take a short position on your stock the next day if they get any sense that you are going to need money, and you'll know exactly who's done it, because you can see what's happening. And when you do bring them to lunch or dinner somewhere, they will, of course, pick the $800 a plate sushi place in Manhattan, and then they have the nerve to go short on your stock the next day and look you in the eye as if there's no problem. That's just something you have to live with.

I remember this happening on our first road show in New York, when one of these funds picked Nobu for lunch, ordering my month's rent right there in front of me! After we said goodbye, we went back over and sat back down and Serguei and I finished the remainder of the $20 per piece sushi, as it wasn't fathomable to let it go to waste when the company was in the financial position that it was..

To give you another example of the game playing, on New Year's Eve of 2021, our stock traded the most amount of shares of any stock in the United States, more than Tesla, Bank of America, Amazon, the lot. Approximately 146 million shares traded on that day, and we ran from

$3 to $12. Now, we had one and a half million shares available to trade at the time. So either every single share traded 100 times, or somebody was naked shorting our stock to try and drive the price down and got caught in a short squeeze.

As of today, certain data that we have shows substantial number has been shorted in our stock since our listing to try and keep it under $5.00. Now I can't say on record that this data is official and accurate, but I can certainly say it fits in very well with our own analysis as to why we see the stock moving as it does, even though we have actually performed quite well since our IPO for the most part. As I understand it, there is really no pressure for these guys to ever cover their short positions unless the stock starts to appreciate dramatically and their risk becomes too high.

The way it works is that most companies like us are in the business of raising money, so if the banks or the funds think you are going back to the market to raise money, they will short your stock down so that you have to raise money at a low valuation. Then they just buy stock back when you go raise money at a low valuation. They make their money off the shorts.

We have made a very conscious effort not to go back and raise money, but we get calls four times a week from banks and funds, offering $10 million, or $30 million, and when we tell them no, it's almost like a shock to them. But we believe there's a huge short position on our stock at time of writing and when it when it finally breaks and it has to be covered, our genuine shareholders will celebrate that day bigtime.

The problem is – and this is an SEC issue again – they should be clamping down on this, because of all the naked shorting on smaller stocks. Somebody will sell a share that they don't ever have, and they'll hide that position in the UK or in Germany. The SEC doesn't have visibility into it (even though they probably do in reality, but they don't do anything about it). So you're constantly fighting this battle of shares flooding the market that actually don't exist. Naked shorting is illegal, but when you legally short a stock you have a period of time to buy that share back to cover, and you have to pay interest on it during the borrow period. But if you naked short it, and you hide it overseas, and you don't ever have to cover the stop.

So, you know, if we have a trading day of 100,000 shares trading, I guarantee maybe about 10,000 of those are a real sale in many cases.

You need a big catalyst. We're going to have to have filings for the FDA approval. That'll start to move the stock, the algorithms will kick in, the funds will start to buy, and as soon as the stock starts to flood upwards, most of those naked shorts will get bought into the market, because the risk manager at the fund won't allow it to go, or the losses would be potentially endless.

That starts flooding the market as well, which creates a short squeeze. So maybe we have a monumental short squeeze on our hands, who can say for sure? I certainly can't go on record confirming it, but I can go on record that I am very confident in the future price of our stock based on what I can see. We just have to make sure we hit our targets with the FDA and continue to hit the targets like we have in the past.

I will state again, however, that these are my opinions and not fact, and that this should not be used as investment advice. I am naturally biased as the CEO, even if the data supports my opinion.

8: Ringing The Bell

Looking back, I have to admit it was a bit strange to be dreaming about making millions when we were living in the in-laws' basement with hardly a cent to our name, with me, supposedly, developing products in the healthcare industry. And then one day I got to have the serious healthcare conversation with the father-in-law.

I asked Heidi's Dad Ned to go grab some lunch one day. So we were sitting there over a cheeseburger at Utah's Crown Burger when I said, "I know I've kind of done things in reverse, but I want to ask your permission to marry Heidi." And he said something like, "Well, you know we love you and everything, and there's not much I can do about it now, she is wearing the ring. But you have my blessing so long as you can afford health insurance. That's the one thing I say to the potential husbands."

We were on Obamacare at the time, and I think I managed to tell him that we'd be fine, that he had my word that she'd have health insurance – not just right then, but that it would definitely happen. So we went back to chatting about things, and that was it, back to living in his basement, promising him I was going give her health insurance, when I couldn't give her a roof over her head.

Right before we had moved back to Utah, we had become friendly with a guy in Ohio called Jason, who just happened to be a jeweller. I was able to negotiate an agreement with Jason to give him 10,000 of my shares in return for an engagement ring. More wheeling and dealing! In fairness, Jason designed and made a cracking ring, worth every hypothetical penny those OTC shares represented at the time.

I told him that those shares were going to be worth a small fortune someday, and he would have to take my word on that, but meantime I needed him to make me a really nice engagement ring so I could actually make things official with Heidi and we wouldn't have to hide it from everyone anymore.

He said "Okay, I trust you, I believe what you're saying." And as it turns out, he has actually done quite well out of it. Those 10,000 shares are worth a lot of money right now but the real value for Jason will be in another year or so hopefully on the news of our approval. So I was able to get a ring made up, but that was the extent of it, due to cash flow issues! In the end the occasion was pretty low key. Heidi always tells me that I'm good at planning things, and "making special occasions," but hey, I was surprised at just how terrible the engagement turned out' in a teasing manner. She'll still give me grief about it a little bit – we often affectionately tease each other and I like that. She is 100% right though, I will admit, it wasn't one of my finer thought-out plans. But it's still the best deal I was ever able to make though!

I remember going and picking up the ring and thinking, *today's the day, I'm going propose.* I called my mum and told her. She said, "As in a marriage proposal? That's so exciting! You know we love Heidi, and you have our support, let us know how it goes." There was a pause, and she said, "But how did you get a ring?" And I said, "Just don't ask..."

When I think back, it was a bit mad. Part of me was thinking, this is so crazy, we're already married! Once again, I found myself looking for pennies between the seats of the car, because obviously the grocery store wasn't going to take shares for chocolates and flowers. But I managed to get a few things, and went back to the apartment, where Heidi was getting ready for a night out. I called her into the kitchen, and she comes in with one eyelash on, her hair is half done, and I'm kind of just shaking on one knee, and I say, "Do you want to marry me again?"

And she kind of laughed and said "yes, of course!" but I knew she was wishing it was all a bit more photogenic. We did go out with friends that night and celebrate with a little bit of money we had put aside, though. That was just before we moved back to her parents' basement, making out we had just got engaged, when they were getting those letters or tax forms addressed to "Mr and Mrs Sheridan".

In the end we weren't in the basement all that long, and we were able to feel like adults again when we moved back to Florida to work seriously on the NASDAQ applications.

The NASDAQ approval to list letter was dated September 28, 2021, and the listing itself occurred on October 1st. The listing was a high point in itself, but we were still feeling the effects of Covid, so there were still lockdowns on and off, which meant that NASDAQ was doing the majority of the bell ringing ceremonies over Zoom, something we weren't keen on. It was such a big moment for us, such a major achievement after such a long, drawn-out process, we didn't want to do it over what would basically be a phone call.

When we put it in our application we were told there was a three-month waiting list, but then on December 1st, I got a call from NASDAQ saying that we were on their cancellation list, and that they'd had a cancellation for the coming Friday, and could we make it?

My immediate thought was, *I'll pull this together! This is happening.* I replied, "Absolutely, we'll be there!" I was going to do it on my own if no one could come, because I wasn't going to pass up the opportunity. It was being offered during a week where it just happened there was no lockdown, and they were doing an in-person bell ringing. I was also thinking, who knows – we're could be in lockdown for the next two years, and we might never get to do a bell ringing. So I confirmed again, "Yes, yes, we'll take it, we'll be there, no problem." And I started making the phone calls.

They had just put up the tree in the Rockefeller Center and New York was starting to look very Christmassy. It was cold, kind of snowy, the lights were going up and it was like the movies when you think of New York, and that just added to the atmosphere of it all.

I did the rest of the phone calls that Wednesday with the team. Whoever could fly in, flew in. My brother, as I mentioned, was the only one unable to make for the ceremony, but celebrated with us that evening. We pulled a pretty strong showing together on very short notice. We probably had 70% of the employees and the executives there. Our lawyers were there, a representative from our investment bank was able to make it, and of course, all the friends and family were in.

The night before, we walked over to Times Square because the NASDAQ is based in Times Square and not Wall Street. We wanted to just take a look at the big screen that we were going to be on, and to take in the environment and the atmosphere of it all.

Afterwards, we all had dinner – some cheap American diner dinner, nothing fancy, just somewhere to be together. I didn't sleep much that night, because this was it, the career pinnacle of anybody who studied business in college and wanted to do that as a career. It's a real milestone to achieve, so it was very exciting.

In the morning we started to get ready for everything. We were all staying in a hotel that was one block over from Times Square. Actually, It was a just an okay hotel in the end, given the circumstances. It was a little run down, having been booked in haste. But that added to it as well, I think, because it made sure people got out and about early and we all walked over together. The location was excellent.

As we walked into the NASDAQ , there was a meet and greet. They give us the royal treatment, a champagne reception. We stayed in the reception area all together and a raised a toast. Then they brought me back to the media room to go through what would happen – that this is where I'd stand, that was what I'd read, and for the countdown, they showed me the button I had to press (it's a bell at the NYSE), and where the ceremony was going to be projected.

So we did a little run through of the proceedings and I practiced my speech, which was going to be projected out on to Times Square live. Then – very quickly – we were doing it for real. It went from practice to two-minute warning, and then we're in count down mode. They put on the big screen and you could see CNBC, Jim Kramer talking, you had Fox business news, and everybody was chatting about the day that was coming up in the stock market.

A woman starts the countdown, counting down from 20 with her hands. I looked up at the screen and all of a sudden I was on CNBC, getting ready to ring the bell, and I was on Fox business – being broadcast on national television all over America – and people are lining up in Times Square to see what is unfolding. Everybody is up on the stage with you – confetti is going all over the place – everybody's cheering and everybody's making a big deal out of it. It's quite surreal.

I felt like I was a bit stiff for most of the time it was happening, because it was just coming from all sides. I felt like everything went into slow motion almost. So much so that I pressed the button twice just to be sure. Maybe it was a subconscious thing, because we had been rejected by NASDAQ twice, so when I pressed that button, I really, really wanted to press it, wanted to slap it down!

Everybody was cheering and having a good time, meanwhile I was just trying to take it all in. I stayed up there for what felt like an eternity, just living the moment. And then they did another countdown – I presume for filming purposes – where we had to keep clapping and cheering as a group until it ended. After that the screens in front of us all switched back to the regular trading sessions, and the national TV went back to normal.

Finally, as the last piece of confetti fell they said, "congratulations, well done, that was great, follow us this way and we'll go back and work on the media pack".

After that, I thought we would be just kind of standing around together discussing it, but they brought us outside into Times Square where we were still being projected, and the big NASDAQ screen read: "Congratulations to Nutriband on opening bell day December 3".

The really interesting thing about this part is the way they cordon off Times Square, and there is a police presence. It was my first taste of what celebrities must go through, because we were in this "reserved" area and everybody was watching and wondering what's going on in there. I mean, we were in the middle of Times Square – there were thousands of people. We were cordoned off having photos taken by a professional photographer, and the police were making sure that nobody came near. We spent about twenty minutes having photos taken as a group, and then they took some of me on my own as CEO for their media pack.

We all took our own photos and selfies as well on our iPhones. Then we were brought back inside for an after reception, where they had more drinks and fingerfood. We stayed there for about an hour or so afterwards so we could mingle and take it all in. I was on such a high that I left my briefcase outside in the Square and one of the police officers had to bring me back out to get it. It had everything in there, and it would have been gone but for him. But I just wasn't thinking, I was overwhelmed by it all.

Back inside we were enjoying ourselves at the reception, and I was already thinking, "This is not the end goal, this is just the beginning." From here on, we would be taking a leap into the bigger leagues and we would have to make sure we execute on everything.

At one point, they gave me a plaque that said "NASDAQ Listing Day," with a few details – something that you hang in your office or put on your desk. But they'd misspelled my name on it. For a second I wondered whether I should say anything about this. Then I realised, I *had* to say something, that I couldn't live with it misspelled for the rest of my life. So I told them about it, and sure enough they brought out a corrected one, which I still have.

Eventually we headed to an Irish pub, had some lunch and tried to absorb it all. Everybody was on a high. My parents were with us, my in-laws, my wife and my brother and his girlfriend showed up later that evening, just in time for that steak at Morton's on 5th Ave.

It was particularly special because they don't allow every company the honour of ringing the bell, you have to meet certain NASDAQ requirements. A lot of NASDAQ companies right now are on the brink of being delisted. You have to maintain a value, you have to have certain equity standards, you have to have assets.

NASDAQ do an opening ceremony and a closing ceremony every day, but a lot of the time the people that ring the opening bell or do the closing bell are charities, who have been given the opportunity as a PR exercise, or you'll have a very large company like Nike back for the ninth time to do it, also as a publicity exercise. A genuine new company probably gets to do it far less often, because I think NASDAQ is quite selective.

That day in Times Square, Nutriband literally opened the NASDAQ market on the same podium, and pressed the same button as some very serious big names had over the years. We were now getting the same treatment and the same visibility. I think that's a lot of it – knowing the calibre of person who's been in that position before you. It's a very nice feeling to be in that group.

They have a good model, and it is the same process over and over. But that doesn't take from the significance of it, the absolute magical experience of it. We had been through so much to get to that point, and that ceremony made it so much better. Being able to get so many of the people that were important to us there on a day's notice from overseas added to the magic. It just came together very nicely, and if I could go back, I wouldn't change a thing.

My parents had a blast, although my mother was a bit emotional. She later told me that at the initial reception, when they brought me out to the rehearsal part and I was walking out with my briefcase with a pep in my step, she was tearing up at that point. She said that watching me being brought into the NASDAQ media room was like watching me the first time she dropped me off at St Joseph's with my schoolbag! It's probably an emotion I will feel someday with my daughter Róe.

My dad is very calm and collected compared to my mother and doesn't express himself in that way. He was there for the party, he just took it all in and enjoyed it, and thought it was all great. The only thing was that he had to keep finding places to sit down because of his back. He can't stand for very long and finds it hard to walk from one point to another. Which is all the more reason for me to keep going with this.

When we were on the OTC, we had reached a $40 million valuation, but you don't really give it much credibility because there's no liquidity in that. It's not accessible. It looks great on paper, but you are only trading 100 or 200 shares in a day.

Overnight, after the NASDAQ listing, you trade thousands of shares in a day, or a million shares. You have the liquidity, so it's a real $40 million. And that is a value that the market has put on it. You are officially and really at that valuation.

We'd got our US patent the day before we listed on the NASDAQ, which was great timing, because now we had people looking at us and we had a press release out that was very strong. We set ourselves the milestone almost straight away to grow the company to a $100 million valuation.

We had started filing patents well before this time, but it is slow, it can drag. When we acquired 4P, they had applications filed but hadn't got the financial means to put pressure on, to keep things moving. We set out to restructure 4P so that we could then concentrate on getting the IP in place.

When I first started going up and down to Atlanta to 4P in late 2018 it was really nice. I had a real office for the first time and they had a boardroom and a lab and all of those things. But this didn't really make financial sense. They were paying something like $17,000 a month in rent and weren't bringing in a whole lot more.

When we looked closely at it, between salaries and equipment they were hardly breaking even, let alone making money. They were very reliant on one or two customers for clinical studies, so if one of those customers left, it would become a big problem.

Don't forget that during this time period, I was still driving an Uber and Serguei had capped himself out. Now suddenly we were looking at this huge space with all this equipment set up that was never used, clean rooms and labs, etc – and we realised that there would be a serious downward trend here if we don't make quick changes.

I have to admit I did feel like a hot shot walking into the lab as the CEO of this company with a clinic, a clean room, a lab, a board room, and all the rest of it. At the time, I didn't know what anything was. I couldn't have told you what any piece of equipment specifically did, but I loved the idea that people might think I did.

When it came to making those necessary changes, one unexpected phenomenon worked to our advantage. It was just at the time when Covid came along, and everyone was going remote, so we were able to change everything at 4P almost under the radar. We shut up shop, put everything in storage, and decided we would outsource the clinical trials to the universities. Now when we look back on it, we can see how these actions saved a huge amount of money and a fortune on rent, without disrupting 4P's ability to make money.

So – remote it was, and that's when we started to get the patents approved regionally. When we got our EU patent, it covered about twenty-seven countries all at once. The UK was included as well, because it was still in its transition period. We jumped from having a couple of patents to more than two dozen patents very quickly, and then we kept adding patents from that point on. We are patented in forty-six countries and regions today and are on all major markets.

It was a completely different story when we acquired Pocono Pharmaceutical, whose company founders had a background in making equipment for Pharma companies. They actually owned their buildings. Additionally, they were sitting on a massive piece of equipment in their inventory which was worth about $2 million all by itself. It was a machine that was originally part of a deal instigated with one of the very big pharma companies, who had changed their minds about the project at the eleventh hour and hadn't moved forward with it, so the guys went ahead and set up Pocono to put the machine to use.

The equipment was very good, and they decided to put it to work by setting it up with a coating capability for sports products. The fact that they built the equipment from scratch meant that we saved a fortune on purchasing that machine ourselves and instead got it through our acquisition of Pocono. The beauty of it was that we were able to start competing with Chinese pricing for US-made products because we weren't paying off the capital cost of a key piece of equipment over ten years.

So now that our pricing was on a par with Chinese competitors, that attracted companies like KT Tape, for example, which is the biggest sports tape brand in the world. That meant we had the right pricing, the manufacturing capability and the "Made in America" stamp, which is very important right now.

I would go out on a limb and say that we're the only company in America that can do what we do against Chinese pricing. The quality is substantially higher, and that's not a dig. You can get great products from China too, and we sometimes purchase machinery or equipment from China and it's great. But the golden goose here – the one that enabled us to compete – was that with Pocono, we were able to get that expensive piece of equipment that a major Pharma company turned down, because they had scrapped the project, essentially for free.

When we acquired them first, they were making sleep patches and similar products, a bit like I was making in the early days. We saw the opportunity to take it on to different level. We thought, "Let's get them registered with the FDA, let's get the current Good Manufacturing Practice (cGMP) Certificate in place, let's make sure that we attract bigger customers." And it started to flow. So now the operation is primarily focused on coatable products that are not on prescription. We do OTC lidocaine patches, kinesiology tapes, sports tapes, that sort of thing.

KT Tape came to us then and so did FFL, who hold the license to Reebok in North America, and they asked us to white label the sports tape products. These days I can walk through a Walmart or a Walgreens or a CVS in the United States, and I'll see products on the shelf that I know have come from our factory. Or I see people wearing or using products that we have made in North Carolina and it's a great feeling.

You can't go around saying, "Hey, we made that product," because some of the big brands don't necessarily want people to know where it was made. So you have to be a well-kept secret in some instances.

The fentanyl patches will be made by Kindeva in California, and we are just going to market the products. There is a particular structure in place there, because fentanyl is a scheduled drug. Kindeva has the licenses, they have the capability to handle it, they have the relationships with the Food and Drug Administration (FDA) and the Drug Enforcement Agency (DEA).

You have to remember that if you're handling fentanyl as an ingredient, the DEA will give you random inspections at any time. And if you're a gram short on what you're supposed to be carrying, it's a shut down the facility situation. So that's not something that I wanted to learn or take on.

So we're partnered with what is probably the number one company in the world with experience of that. We will never have to physically touch or hold the product that we're selling, and neither do we want to. It will go straight to the distribution network that already exists, in a highly safe and controlled manner.

We've done a lot of the heavy lifting already in terms of our FDA filing for approval. The way our trials are structured is more simple than a typical, "Phase one, two, three" type of clinical development plan.

Because we're taking a product that already exists, and making improvements upon that, we only have to do one single "phase one" clinical trial, which is a human abuse liability study. In simple terms, we give our patch and a generic patch to a controlled room of recreational opioid abusers with a high tolerance and monitor which one can be abused or which one the participants are more likely to attempt to abuse.

You may ask, is this even legal, but it's a necessary evil. The conditions are very controlled, and the people in the trial are already opioid users. I think it's fairly self-evident that they're going to look for ways to abuse the one that has no safety mechanism built in over ours, which has.

When we get the results of that trial, we'll be able to state 'Abuse Deterrent' on the label, which sets us apart from all of our competition. It's also a branded product, which doesn't fall into the generic category, so it's not transferable or interchangeable with generics or competitors' products from an insurance perspective. We can lock in a price and it can't be transferred to a competitor.

We also had to do non-clinical feasibility studies, proving that our technology works. What we are doing hasn't been done before. It sounds simple, just spray the ingredients to the back of the fentanyl patch and away you go, people won't use them. But the science, the know-how and the equipment to do that has thus far not existed – this has not been done before. You have to make sure that the products have a shelf life, and will have enough of a deterrent effect, that they do not seep into the fentanyl layer, that the fentanyl is delivered in the correct amounts, that the patch will perform correctly. There are many aspects to it, and these are all the non-clinical studies that had to be done.

We had been doing all of this for quite some time when we realised we needed a third-party vendor to provide the backing layer because Kindeva were not set up to do that. We've been working on finding the right vendor that has the capability in what is a difficult supply chain. That's been quite a hurdle. There are only so many companies in the world that can actually do it. We now have the company sourced, and we will be in a position shortly to start the human abuse liability study. That trial will last approximately three months and when we have the results we'll work to package the final submission for the FDA with the rest of our data. It's a platform approach. A lot of the work we're doing on this first product can then be reused on product number two, or product number three.

We had hoped to have our New Drug Application (NDA) submission in by now, but it is typical of drug development that you come across hurdles, unforeseen events and delays. Things that seem easy and simple will sometimes cause shareholders to ask, well how hard is it?

It is hard. Because these are people's lives at the end of the day, and you have to have everything done very precisely. The other key thing is that you really only get one shot with the FDA. If they look at it, and it appears that you rushed it, or that you cut corners, you will be looked at unfavourably.

So I would rather take an extra six months and get it right, than try, fail – and need to start over again, having to rename the company and the product, and all of that, which is something that you see happening.

A huge amount is hanging on the FDA, but I'm very confident that we will get an approval. As a company, I think we're very secure in our position. Kindeva has recently restructured our agreement to a point where they are going to charge us less, but will take a small royalty on the products. They are confident that the products are going to go to market, and they are going to get a better percentage return in the long term.

We reached out to the FDA regarding a pre-IND meeting (IND stands for "Investigational New Drug"). The pre-IND and IND meetings are a bit like going to your local authority and asking for a pre-planning meeting before you submit plans for a new house. It's where we tell them what we plan to submit, and how our trials are laid out, and ask whether there is anything else they want us to do.

We can also seek advice related to the development and review of our submission. The IND meeting is essentially a request for authorisation to use the unapproved drug in trials and administer it for the purpose of data collection. We'll be targeting to file for approval in the fourth quarter of 2025.

I see a $500 million company valuation as the next milestone. It's not unreasonable to think that we'll get there on the back of the approval. That was the growth trajectory we saw from the start, and it is moving closer to its goal all the time. The most recent milestone in the journey is the addition of the patent approval in China, covering us fully worldwide from a patent perspective. All major markets are now there for the taking.

9: Zoom Courtroom and a Victory

The first house Heidi and I managed to buy was in Utah, following the other company acquisitions, and the steadying of the Nutriband Inc ship. It was a very old house and a very small house, about the size of a two-bed apartment.

It had a scary old unfinished basement with lots of wood panelling and an old boiler system. Interestingly, there was also a fully-plumbed, raised toilet out in the open with no walls or fixtures, just sitting there like a throne. When Serguei came to visit one time and saw it, he took a picture and said, "This is going to be a great story one day when you look back at this office."

It was dingy and a bit grungy, but I bought a desk that was falling apart on Craigslist from some lady for about $40 and that was the set up. I thought it looked pretty good and was fairly pleased with myself. It was a lot better than a laptop on your knee in a Starbucks somewhere or working in a corner of an Airbnb.

I still have a picture of the old Asus laptop, where the space bar is smashed up. I'm not an aggressive person or anything, but after one of the many negative events we went through, I actually slammed the keyboard, and the spacebar suffered badly.

So getting that little house was a big progression for us at that point. It actually turned out very well in the end and we still own it, we have let it out. Maybe we will eventually give to Róe, as her inheritance.

We took a hammer to the walls and tried to open it all up. But when I say small, it was really, really small. I'm six foot seven, so I need a bit of space. The kitchen just about fitted a cooktop and a fridge, so we were scooting around each other all the time whenever we were in there.

But we changed it around and eventually it even got to where we actually quite liked it. It was ours, and it was home, despite having been a construction site for so long. We lived in it for a couple of years, and I thought that the basement office was just great. It was private and quiet, and I could do my calls. I had a sheet tacked up across the wall, and I put up a whiteboard (which I never used), and a few other bits and pieces, just to make the background look professional for Zoom calls. It worked just fine. We had upsized by 2022, and I had upgraded my office substantially by the time the Advanced Health appeal decision came through.

Judge Rodriguez, you will recall, said at the time that he didn't want a reversal on his last case before he retired, and I even remember him making a big R symbol with his hand, right there in the courtroom, hammering home to us that this wasn't going to happen. Several years had passed by now, as the case made its way through the system.

For context, when we sued, we had sued to rescind the agreement between ourselves and Advanced Health, so the parties would go back to exactly how they were originally. That meant that we would have no relationship or partnership whatsoever, and everyone would take back what they owned prior to our agreement. The court order from Judge Rodriguez, the judgement, was that the contract was to proceed and go ahead as agreed, and they were to assign the patents back to us.

But the immediate argument from us was that neither party was asking for that. When it has gone as far as a lawsuit, a judge can't just decide to mediate and try to make things how they deem to be fair. We appealed it on the basis that the court decision was rendered in favour of nobody essentially, because nobody asked for that solution.

I remember our attorneys saying they couldn't understand the position the judge was coming from because it's not how the law works. If you sue for something, you either get it or you don't. You don't expect a judge to come back to say, "Let's all play happy families here, let bygones be bygones, and why don't you just ignore the fact that they have proven themselves to be untrustworthy and fraudulent, and carry on as before?"

By this stage it was not just the shares and the patents that were in question. We would have been locked into bed with people that we could not trust, and that huge factor was completely disregarded by the judge.

And of course the cherry on top for Advanced was that they got to keep our $50,000 bond. It was like Judge Rodriguez had completely favoured them, despite what he had heard in court. We knew we needed to get it under another judge's eyes.

We came up with a game plan. We filed the appeal immediately in Florida, and then we filed an additional lawsuit in Ohio, just to tie them up some more. It's an unfortunate aspect of the system, but we felt that if we filed a lawsuit in Ohio as well, maybe it would put more financial pressure on them, because they'd have to hire attorneys and defend it there too. So we became quite aggressive with it – we had no choice – and put together a very strong appeal, which we filed. We had listed on the NASDAQ towards the end of the discovery, so we had the arsenal to go at it full swing to get a huge chunk of our now NASDAQ-listed company back. The shares they held had a liquid value in the millions of dollars at this point.

There was months and months of hearing nothing until finally a new judge was assigned and the process started over. That was somewhere around the start of Covid so much of it had to be done over Zoom. A very close friend of mine was getting married at the time of the hearing, and I was in France for the wedding. So while Serguei was able to do some of the court appearances in person, I attended all the hearings fully over Zoom. For example, the day before my friend's wedding, I was sitting on a bed in the hotel, wearing a shirt and tie, being questioned for six hours by the attorneys on the other side who were throwing everything at me!

I was a bit more rehearsed this time, I think. I had been through a court process several times by then, and the SEC process, and so wasn't as freaked out by it this time around. They do try to catch you, they try to make you slip up, they try to take quotes out of context. But

I was definitely better able for it this time, and I think I performed quite well. Heidi just sat there with her popcorn listening in, actually enjoying the show. And then we went off to the wedding eve party.

We were back in Utah when we got word that we had we won, and even if it was three years later, it was quite something, because the judge found in our favour this time around. He didn't try to mediate a solution that nobody asked for. And we won on absolutely all counts. "Congratulations" was the first word in all my emails, and I didn't have to go much further than that! I remember thinking, "Here we go, just perfect."

I read the judgement fully then, and it was clear that it wasn't just a bit of a win, or a slight win. Every single thing came our way. It was over, and it was such a great feeling to put all that behind us. We were able to take back control of approximately 15% of the company's stock, which had been a constant worry for so long. They received their IP back as part of the judgement, which wasn't difficult to finalise seeing as it was already in their name, and we didn't need it, as we had developed our own IP by then. We parted ways and never spoke directly again.

We had to prepare for the chance that they might counter appeal, however, but we came to an agreement that we would not sue them for our legal fees, which at this time was in the hundreds of thousands of dollars, If they just let it go, we could all walk away.

I think by the end of it they were financially spent on this lawsuit, because the hot-shot attorney that they had at the beginning was now just cc'd on emails and an associate attorney was on the case, who wasn't as good. In the end there was no follow up appeal, we cut our losses on the legal fees, and we got back what was rightfully ours. Our next thought was how to reward the shareholders for their patience.

All you ever see in our space is reverse splits. For example, if your stock drops below a dollar, you're in a de-listing territory with NASDAQ. So a lot of companies will do, let's say, a ten for one reverse split. That means, if your shares are at fifty cents, you now have one share for every ten shares you had, but that share is five dollars. So there's not an immediate effect on the value of your holdings, but when you do a reverse split, it has a snowball effect – it will slip straight back down below a dollar again. It's a kind of a death spiral. Reverse splits are not perceived very well on the street. It looks like the company's in trouble. We've never done a reverse split on NASDAQ and we don't ever plan to.

The way we looked at it, everybody around us was doing reverse splits and it was killing companies. We decided to announce a forward split. So we did a seven for six forward split to the value of the shares we recouped in the deal. That meant for every six shares a shareholder had, they now had seven. The stock price drops accordingly at first, but because you've done a forward split, it starts to naturally progress back up again. And people can gain.

When you announce a forward split, it's usually done about month before you actually execute the split. So you get people saying, "These guys are going to do a forward split, I'm going to buy this stock and hold it for the free share."

It's a very positive thing to do. The big guys – the "Magnificent Seven" do forward splits – Apple, Amazon and so on. Netflix will probably do a forward split in late 2025 in my opinion. So it was good to be able to do that, to create a buzz. It's like the market is saying, "these guys are doing a forward split, these guys are confident in the company."

It was definitely a reward for people who'd stuck with us. We had shareholders who had stayed with us throughout the SEC troubles and throughout the lawsuits, and we owed them. It was a way to make it clear that we are very shareholder-focused. I think that has become a characteristic of Nutriband that people are more aware of now. We all see the value in the stock, and where it can go, and in trying to be as non-dilutive as possible.

So what better way to be non-dilutive than to be the opposite of dilutive, and actually issue more shares to shareholders? The whole move was very well received, the stock jumped, going up to $7 a share at that point and definitely creating a bit of buzz. That brought in a new following, and eyes on us as well with all the news coverage. So it was nice to be able to pull it off.

When you become a public company, you give away a certain control over who owns your shares. We have never gotten to a position where one individual, worrying shareholder has gone over ten percent, which would give them a higher influence on board decisions and votes etc.

We're interested in following the funds that start to pick us up. So if we see Vanguard, Bank of America or Merrill Lynch, these type of funds and investment banks, start to build a position with us, that's actually nice to see. But these are the type of funds that don't want to come in and take over control of the company. That's not their business.

If I was in the airline industry and I saw that Michael O'Leary or Ryanair had suddenly accumulated 15% of my company, I'd be a bit nervous. But we're not really in that sort of league or that realm. What typically happens in Pharma is not a hostile takeover. It's usually a situation where guys come in with a big chequebook and offer to take over.

Obviously, there are eyes on us now the closer we're getting to an FDA submission. It's getting more interesting for the market. Another thing to keep under consideration is that these funds typically don't invest in anything under five dollars. I think there's actually an SEC rule on that.

So five dollars is a threshold for the big boys to come in and take positions. Another rule is that a major fund, for compliance purposes, can only trade a certain percentage of the volume for the month. So we have had periods where we're only trading ten or fifteen thousand shares on average in a month, it's not worth their while to buy fifteen or twenty percent of that. These guys like to build positions.

This year and last year, we've had great liquidity, and we've started to see that slowly trickle up. But we're still under 10% ownership on an institutional level.

You have to be wary of certain funds that might build a position, and which are known to short stocks. So we keep an eye on that as well. We've had that in the past, but it has reduced substantially as we built more credibility and hit targets. There is such a clear difference when you list on NASDAQ with the liquidity it brings, compared to the OTC markets.

I love to follow it and see who's building positions, who's not building positions, and you know, if you want to short our stock right now, you're more than welcome to try. In my confidently biased opinion once again, it's only going to add fuel to the fire when we run and when we hit our milestones.

We got some unofficial data from an independent analyst in 2024 who looked at our short set up, that says there's something like $2 billion short in our stock since we listed. The company's worth a hundred million, and the short amount, according to this guy, is $2 billion. Now whether his algorithm and mathematics are completely accurate, who knows, but I am a believer that when dealers get forced to cover any short positions, there's not going to be enough shares available to buy. So it's a GameStop moment in the making perhaps. But who knows – I can't say for sure – we'll have to see how it plays out.

You have to learn to read it from a psychological perspective, not just by the numbers. It's not just the passion for it, or how you might feel. You have to be sensible and you have to picture the worst-case scenario. It goes back to that example I mentioned before when a guy wanted to come in with $1m in the early days. I thought it was perfect, and that it was really going to help us. But we had to say no, otherwise in a few years' time we would have been at fifty cents a share.

You try to look beyond the immediate good feeling on things. The real rule of thumb is that nobody is going to let you make millions of dollars on Wall Street if they can help it, let alone a billion which is what we have our sights on. You have to do it yourself, and you have to do it at someone else's expense. There's winners and losers, and for somebody to win, somebody else has to lose. That may be somebody who is shorting our stock, and we win on the back end. Or we announce a reverse split for our shareholders, and they win. It's a free trading market.

I would say I'm a trusting person, but I'm always questioning the angle you're coming from. When I meet with an investment bank, I will play happy family, I will be friends, and I come away from the meetings wondering, if I follow the stock now will I see them try to short it? I don't come away saying, "Oh, they might buy our stock and it's going to run."

It is a weird dynamic, but it's not a personal one. As I said before, it's almost like a game and you're trying to beat your high score every week. That was the biggest thing I had to learn, whereas the thing that took the longest time to learn was to not take things personally.

I definitely wear a harder shell when I'm in New York on Wall Street and having those conversations, but I think I've become quite a good judge of character, and that dictates a lot of it these days. The overarching thing to remember with investment bankers is that quite often they are not your friends. So by going into the meeting with that in the back of my mind, I can play ball, I can go to lunch, but I know that if they can make money at my expense, they will. But so can I, at theirs.

Now that's not to say all bankers are like this, we actually do have good banking relationships with larger firms that we believe are genuine supporters of the company. These would be firms that are typically outside of the microcap dealers we were used to in our early days, firms that it's very nice to know are paying attention to us now and will credit us on escaping the pits of Wall Street by sticking to our strategy and not following the easy cash.

We have developed relationships with a number of investment bankers over the years, and there are one or two in particular, whom Serguei hasn't got a lot of time for. But they would often reach out to me informally over WhatsApp or email to check on the company and naturally ask if we needed money, and while I know that it's likely they shorted our stock, it's part and parcel of their playbook. I don't trust many investment bankers, but would I go to lunch with them if they asked me when I'm in New York? Sure. They might have some useful information for me. Would I buy a used car from one of them? Probably not.

I'm often asked why we went for the NASDAQ and not the New York Stock Exchange, and honestly, I wouldn't rule out the New York Stock exchange at some point in my career for the prestige. But the NASDAQ is definitely more receptive to younger, high-growth tech companies. Most biotech companies like ours are listed on the NASDAQ. So if we want to have the attention of investors that are focused on those sort of companies, the NASDAQ makes most sense.

The NYSE is harder to get started on. They're a bit more snobby about applications, more traditional. In terms of trading volume, NASDAQ is actually bigger, but New York has the prestige of being The New York Stock Exchange. Technically it is not higher up the ladder, but still, you would always look at it as the prime exchange. The companies that listed in the golden era are all on the New York Stock Exchange, the old industrial type of US companies – General Motors and the like. So you would definitely be among all the old big names.

But the biotech pharma companies and the tech companies are definitely all NASDAQ. Facebook is on NASDAQ, for example, and out of what they call the Magnificent Seven companies, five of them are on the NASDAQ. It's a different clientele in a way, and I suppose a personal preference. So it made more sense for us to be a NASDAQ company. We wouldn't be trading at anything more if we were on the New York.

As a business student, you think of hitting the bell with a hammer, and the old-style New York trading floor. That's definitely what you think of. The NASDAQ isn't like that, it's all digital. You press a button when you 'ring the bell', there are no traders on the floor. It's more like a media studio.

I've done the tour of the New York Stock Exchange with a firm we were working with, and I'll admit to feeling giddy in there, because you do see the traders, you do see CNBC being filmed live. It's the real deal. I have pictures of myself up on the New York ceremonial stage holding the hammer and yes, I definitely felt at home.

A question I get asked a lot is whether I'm looking to sell out, whether we might be acquired. It's not something I'm seeking or that I give too much thought to, and of course we have already had those calls, people feeling us out so see if we are open to an acquisition. It's not something we'd entertain right now, particularly as we're so close to executing on the big plan. Our goal right now is that this could be a multi-generational company. If we pull it off, and we do it right, our grandchildren could inherit the company and continue to do what we started. That's a realistic scenario.

On the other hand, if somebody came in with a cheque book and offered big money, it's ultimately not up to me, or not up to Serguei, or not up to the board. It's actually up to the shareholders. If a majority of the shareholders decide that they like that price, then the company will be sold. You lose control from that aspect as a public company.

But I believe our shareholders are aligned. Our top five shareholders control about 65% of the company, and as of now, we're all of the same mindset. So when I say I'm not overly worried about that right now, I retain full awareness of the fact that everybody has their price.

10: A New Family Member

The reality about the unique partnership that led to all of this is, I think, that Serguei was a capital markets guy – his experience was in public markets and public companies, and he was looking for a really strong fit to list as a public company. I would say I was probably the driver of the idea to form a public company, but we wanted to do it in a socially correct but game-changing way.

It wasn't a joint vision that we had out the gate, it was a growth-filled process with tweaks and adjustments made as we went, but I think it landed perfectly. Serguei leans on me for the business and science side of Pharma, and I lean on him for the public side of things.

I had one very negative early experience with public markets already under my belt, but the point that Serguei hammered home to me from an early stage was that this was only going to work if we were completely aligned. At any point, one of us could have derailed it for the other, made a quick buck and moved on. But we're now coming up on ten years in partnership, and all going well, we'll both make substantially more money than we would ever have made individually, because there has been trust and an understanding there.

In terms of being a patient-focused Pharma company, we have grown into this. But I am reminded of it every day by my dad. The relentless pain he deals with on a daily basis reminds me that he's only one of thousands and thousands of people who are experiencing this, and it makes me want to keep going to change things for them. It helps too, that all down the years, my parents kept saying, "Keep at it, don't give up," despite how they must have felt at certain stages of it, I am sure.

When that *Sunday Business Post* article came out, with the $100 million valuation on the company, my mum sent it to all the family on WhatsApp. But that's no different to when they shared articles the press ran about my winning the start-up awards in 2014. They loved those articles and yes, they showed them off a little, but they are not one bit braggy or showy or boastful.

They're never going to say, "Our son's company is worth X, let's go buy a Mercedes." Nothing's changed for them. They will be the exact same on the good days as they were when we got our NASDAQ rejections. They're just there for us, and really happy that we're making a living where we can take care of Róe and we're happy. That's their thing.

They now have another son to share press articles on WhatsApp about: my brother Aaron. He's the tech-head and is starting to be recognised as a bit of a talent in the space with awards and acknowledgments now too. He is well versed in blockchain and tech and things I generally don't understand, that will likely drive technologies of the future. I think the thought of AI as it continues to grow in the Pharma and diagnostics space is very interesting, so maybe we will work together on something down the line, combing our expertise.

Family is very important to me, and the story of how Róe came into our lives is worth the telling. Heidi's mother Kathy is one of the directors of The Adoption Exchange in Utah, now known as 'Raising the Future,' one of the biggest non-profit adoption charities there. Heidi has ten siblings, eight of whom were also adopted. In the course of our relationship together, Kathy had often asked us whether adopting a child was something we would ever consider. We'd always say, no, "It's not something we've really thought about."

But then a family member of Heidi's became pregnant and wasn't in a position to be a mother at that time for her own reasons. So we offered to help out with minding Róe, until the family figured out the situation.

We were all trying to do our bit. So we offered to have Róe come and stay for a while with us. So there we are, Heidi and I and this fraction of a human about 10 inches tall trying to figure out life together. Heidi and I just looking at each other every so often reading each others' mindset and discussing options. Heidi and Róe developed a bond very fast, Heidi has always been great with children. Then one day very quickly after she arrived, she just reached out and held my finger – and that was it for me. In my head, I said, "Where's the papers?"

That was all it took – the moment when she held my finger, which I know all babies do, but not all babies do it to you! It was just a magical moment. Heidi and I exchanged a look between us, and we instantly knew she was one of us, and now I am the one wrapped around Róe's finger. The girl knows how to play me.

Just before that, we had been thinking that we might have just played the role of the cool aunt and uncle; that we wouldn't have any kids of our own. And it was almost as if the universe or a higher power said, "Well, let's put that to the test." We never got to prepare for it, we never went through the pregnancy period or the anticipation of having a child. We were told there was a new baby in the family one day, and then very quickly we had taken Róe in and we were trying to figure out how to be parents. I suppose diving in at the deep end and learning from mistakes was similar to the early days with Nutriband!

It was really natural, we all made a decision pretty quickly, although it took about a year to get through the full adoption process. We were considered as foster parents at first, a "kinship" I think it was called, so we had monthly inspections from the case workers to make sure that we were doing okay as parents and that she was doing well with us.

I had conference in London a short time later and we took Róe with us. I called my mum – who didn't get to prepare either, she was just told she was going to be a grandmother – and asked her if she'd meet us in London. She took to Róe immediately, and there was instant bond. Then she stayed on a few days to help us.

We finished the conference in London and then we travelled home to Ireland for about two months, so

Róe could meet and get to know everybody and get integrated into my family. It was quite simple, actually, in terms of her being allowed to travel and stay in Ireland, as she is entitled to citizenship through me, which we are working on. With Heidi, it's a little trickier. She has to be a resident for some time before that happens.

The main challenge that we had to deal with when we flew to Ireland with Róe for the first time was that she still had a different surname from us, since the adoption was not yet finalised. But we were able to get a clearance from the Court in Salt Lake City. We had specifically asked them to provide us with a document that stated we were allowed to travel with her, as we were still in the adoption process. So that's what we had to provide everywhere we went at that time. The immigration officer would look at it, sometimes they would check it with the supervisor, who would then sign off on it, and it would be fine.

The process did eventually, as we'd been told, take a year. There is a minimum period that you have to go through, even with a family adoption, before the papers can be signed off on. But finally one day, my parents flew over, Heidi's parents were there, and we went to the courthouse to finalise the formalities.

It was such a happy day, and such a happy outcome for everyone, and it just so happened to be her first birthday – so right afterwards we were able to have her birthday party with everyone there, and celebrate together. It's turned out to be very good part of our already unconventional story, and it happened very naturally.

In one of the photos from that day, Róe is looking at me very intently, with a finger pointing outwards, like an athlete would do when they're saying they're number one. When I posted it on to the family feed, someone commented on it, saying, "it was meant to be!" Parenthood changes everything for you.

She's two and a half now, and an absolute lunatic. She says the funniest of things and we have no idea where she's picked them up from, although we have our suspicians every time we go over to Nana's house and hear some similar phrases like 'Janey Mack'. I find myself anticipating when the new season of 'Cocomelon' is going to drop on Netflix so we can watch it together. Last season left us on a clifhanger, were JJ and Cody going to finish the sand castle or not?

I can't say our daughter was an angel from the beginning – the lack of sleep thing was a nightmare. Heidi did 95% of the work, because it was right after our last listing phase, and I was struggling with that. Heidi was a trooper again, as with everything we'd already been through. She took on the role of mother as if she were made for it.

So now I was no longer the entrepreneur in his late twenties running around the place any more. I became that dad of a two-year-old with the compounding savings account already set up for her, and wondering whether she'll go to Harvard. It makes you grow up very quickly, in one way you mature overnight, which I think has probably had a very positive impact on the business as well. It makes you realise you don't need the parties and the socialising so much. Movies and lighting a fire and going to bed at nine are great too, and I'd never have imagined that such a change could happen in the space of six months.

I mentioned before how hard it was to make all the phone calls to people when we got the second rejection from NASDAQ, since at that time we had been one hundred percent certain that the calls were going to be celebratory.

There was one call I was petrified to make, and that was to Dave, the man who invested the first big money in the company. He was expecting a return that year, and I was going to have to tell him that he would be waiting at least another year. But thankfully he had always understood and been supportive of me, even though I'm sure he, like many others, wondered if I was a dreamer at times.

Just a few months ago, as I was arriving in Orlando for our annual shareholder meeting, I heard someone behind me say, "All right big man?" I turned around and there was Dave, whom I hadn't seen in person in about three years. For a moment I thought he was coming to the shareholder meeting, but he was on a layover on the way to Mexico.

The coincidence was like a good omen for the shareholder meeting, because it turned into the best shareholder meeting we've ever had. It was great to see Dave, and our conversation was pleasant and reassuring, which meant a lot to me. If no one else was ever to make a return on their investment with us, I would make sure that Dave got his return, because the company wouldn't be anywhere close to where it is today without his belief in us, and the risk he took. There are certain people like that, who we encountered along the way – and I'd put Joe D, the attorney, in there too – and they are in the inner circle of untouchables. They will be looked after.

As I look now to the future, and how the world is moving, we have to keep growing and developing the business, and trying to make a difference where we can, both economically and socially.

11: Back In The Parish

So here we are back in Dublin, home again and it's great to be back in the parish and on our own terms. Meeting up with friends again, in person, not just online. You'd miss the slagging. Heidi is loving it too; Róe is in her element and my folks are over the moon. As a family, we've definitely made the right decision, the best decision. We're not home a wet week – the Irish weather --and we're already making plans to visit our family Stateside later in the summer.

Heading out to work the other morning Róe didn't want me to go, but to stay and play with her. It is a great feeling. But I was almost late for my meeting with the traffic in Donnybrook and the parking in town. It seems things are like that these days.

Heidi did an interview and the papers loved her. She made the front of *The Mirror* and also got a big splash in *The Star*, *The Sunday World*, and *The Independent* – lots of interest in her work as an interior designer and a model, and our return back to Ireland as a family.

She's got some really interesting ideas in the pipeline herself, and more media attention on the way. Things are shaping up great.

At the same time, I've been doing these rounds of non-stop interviews with the BBC, RTE, *Newstalk*, *The Sunday Business Post* and all kinds of media. The whole world seems convulsed and at a standstill, with everyone holding their breath to see what a tariff trade war will unleash. Almost 3 trillion was wiped off the stock markets at the beginning of April, the stock sell-off the worst trading since the Covid pandemic.

Thankfully, Nutriband is holding up well amid the chaos, but of course it concerns me. We're listed on the NASDAQ. The Magnificent Seven are taking a hammering and I read that in preparation for potential tariffs with China, Apple flew five commercial airplanes full of iPhones into the US as a contingency plan. And yet in all the frenzy about stocks, shares, values, investments, tariffs and trade wars, I'm here in Dublin thinking this is about a lot more than just car parts and Harley Davidsons.

Pharma is thankfully spared in the first tranche of tariffs. Maybe someone in the political circles, somewhere heard my message these past few weeks and is seeing some sense. This is about people's meds, and without wanting to be alarmist, we're talking chemotherapy and diabetes treatments, with Ireland at the heart of the storm.

I got a great opportunity in a radio interview with Pat Kenny to explain how pharmaceutical tariffs are far more complicated than the narrative is suggesting lately. Ireland has been slowly and steadily building the pharmaceutical industry for fifty years now. It is successful here because of the infrastructure, the innovation and the people. This is not something that can be easily undone and re-routed in a couple of weeks or months. Ultimately I believe that the discussion of pharma tariffs will make it difficult to attract future investment in Ireland, at least for now, but we should use this opportunity to our advantage also and look at new industries, look to tech, AI and all of the exciting emerging spaces where I know Ireland can add benefit and continue to grow.

I was recently selected as a finalist for the EY Entrepreneur of the Year awards. It was a great feeling to get the phone call that I made it into the shortlist, I am very excited to meet all of the excellent entrepreneurs and see the amazing ideas that continue to flow out of this impactful little island. We are off to Japan as a group at the end of May for a "Finalists retreat" for what I imagine will be a very memorable trip.

It's been so busy since we got home but I'm loving it, relishing it, embracing it. Reconnecting with old friends, meeting new people, playing a bit of football again, even if the legs are gone. I'm seeing and engaging with a whole new range of possibilities and opportunities – it's really exciting. There is so much to be positive about in Ireland today, but on the other hand I've come to appreciate that there are a lot of problems that we can't ignore too.

The cost of living in Dublin has gone through the roof and as for the price of houses, how did we let that happen? At one end of the scale, the Swedish Embassy decided to rent their premises, since the cost of purchasing was so expensive. How can a recent graduate read that headline and feel positive about purchasing a home of their own any time soon if Sweden couldn't? On the other hand the Department of Housing is reporting that we have more than 15,000 homeless people in the country. How did we not foresee this and have a plan in place? There is such a problem with the lack of housing that it overshadows the fact that we also have a major problem with homelessness.

I attended a seminar for approved housing bodies in the Dublin offices of law firm Addleshaw Goddard just off Baggot Street recently where one of the keynote speakers was Priya Nair, Chief Executive of The Housing Finance Corporation in the UK. Something she said about the complexity and issues around providing more homes really struck a chord with me.

"The scale of the challenge requires partnerships. What we are doing is foundational in every sense. It's about more than just bricks and mortar, it's about social cohesion, social responsibility and sustainability as we seek to create a positive impact in all that we do. That remains our 'North Star'". I took that away with me. I want to build on that.

Ireland is full of great innovation, the best people, the extraordinary history, the captivating culture and landscapes and is really one of the best places to live in the world, if you can afford to.

America was very good to us as a family and especially for Nutriband. One day, I was at a working lunch in Lennon's on Dawson Street and was asked what I miss about the States, and I said, our friends, Beto's Burritos, In'n'Out Burger, and drive through pharmacies, which are many simple conveniences that America offers for day to day life. I was almost eaten alive. Because there's lots of great burritos in Dublin, and restaurants to die for, so much good stuff going on here too. If only my age group who are putting in the hours, making the effort and want to live here, could afford a decent home without having to pay an arm and a leg for it, and put themselves into debt for the rest of their lives. This is one of the things that is really hitting home with me.

We're settling in, enjoying the simple things like taking Róe to the park – Heidi and I are buzzing with our ideas and plans. I'm off to a Leinster match in Croke Park with the lads and, contrary to the urban myths, we'll be shouting for Munster afterwards against the old foe, La Rochelle. We owe them one, or two! I'm also on the lookout for a couple of tickets for Electric Picnic as I am a big Hozier fan and I really want to take Heidi to see him in Stradbally.

I am very aware that I'm blessed and have been lucky in the Nutriband journey, so much so that we are part of a small group who have been fortunate to be able to afford to move home these days. Continuing the dream, here in Dublin, Ireland. A few of us went to the O2 Arena to see Shane Gillis, and we had a great night out. He's a big favourite these days. And again, with all the positives that come with returning home and settling back in, there's stuff frustrating me too.

Society in the US is far from perfect, as my father-in-law Ned will attest, having recently raised a Canadian flag outside the house, where it will stay for the next 4 years. But it's clear that we have our fair share of problems here as well. All major economies like Ireland and the US have such challenges – they are part of navigating growth, but it's how you prepare for and tackle those problems that sets you apart and defines you. Thirteen years ago, Leo Varadkar described the housing situation in Ireland as a national emergency, and then it was officially declared an emergency in 2017. And when I look at what's happened since that time, and ask myself what has been done about it – the answer appears to be, "absolutely nothing."

It's very disheartening for my generation and it impacts everything else as well, like education, healthcare, climate change and emigration to name a few – it's about so much more than having a roof over your head, a home is the foundation for so much. It makes you wonder if our next generation will be able to stay here at all, our daughter Róe included.

We should not be surprised that Ireland has become a country where people want to live, a country where people look to now for opportunity, and as a result a country that should have foreseen the need in infrastructure long ago.

I read recently that banks have lent less and less every year since the crash in 2008 and I cannot understand the psychology behind this. We also have a planning system fit for The Flintstones. How can we attract international investment in our infrastructure when our own banks look unconfident and investors can't expect a return for a decade because of the pointless red tape in the planning system? While industries, tech, pharma and innovation have all grown in the last ten years, our infrastructure to house this growth has lagged, to the point where we will be playing catch up for some time unless someone stops talking and starts doing.

During Storm Éowyn, which was in full force as we were moving back into Dublin, we kept hearing about all the repair teams who were brought in from abroad to help restore power. Many homes around the country had no power for up to ten days, and it struck me that that many of our own electricians are in fact working in Manhattan or Melbourne because they can't afford houses at home.

This is at a time when the government has more money in the coffers than ever before, yet nobody seems to have the will to sort out the problem. I hear the latest hot topic is a three-billion-euro budget to buy fighter jets and military equipment and meanwhile you think that same three billion euro would build approximately 12,000 homes.

Meanwhile grandparents have to settle for seeing their grandchildren in Toronto or Sydney on an iPad on Sunday afternoons, hoping and praying for the day when they can afford to visit them and give them a hug. You meet people out on a Friday night in Brooklyn who will tell you they haven't seen their mother in ages, or they have never met their little niece, or they have missed out on the first communions and the weddings and the football finals and even the funerals.

The truth is, of course, that Irish people like to travel and see the world and have a great time and gain brilliant experience, the adventure is a great part of our culture. But I think most of them see it as temporary, they see themselves returning and settling at home, and it is very disappointing when they don't have that choice, because if they come home, they'll have nowhere to live. That year abroad becomes two, and then three, and then four...

What's the point of even talking about supporting the arts if parish halls and local theatres have no audiences to buy tickets, and no one is around to act in the plays? What's the point in banging on about sports facilities when the players are living abroad... That's one of the reasons our hospital wards and emergency rooms lack doctors, nurses and health care professionals – because they literally cannot find affordable places to live near the hospitals and clinics!

Which brings me to the other reason why medical professionals are taking up properly paid jobs in Calgary and Sydney instead of Dublin or Galway: the broken state of our healthcare and hospital system.

It's another gigantic, wheezing elephant in the room that is not going away, and yet successive administrations have failed to address the health service. In a country with one of the most technologically capable populations in Europe, and now the most expensive hospital building in the world, there is no comprehensive digitised computer system that can record the health details of its population, making crucial case histories available to cross-reference between the departments of each hospital – let alone across different hospitals and emergency rooms. Simple things that America does well, in contrast.

I just don't get it, how we could build so many houses, both public and private, in the 60s and 70s, when we were an economic basket case, and now when our economy is one of the highest-performing in the world, we are destroying hope by not providing housing, and allowing a situation where sick people are left neglected on trolleys in emergency room corridors. Some of the stories in the media over the past few years have been nothing short of horrific.

And don't get me started on the salaries! I know people in their thirties who did stay home, and didn't go abroad, and they can't move out of their parents' back bedroom, or get married, or start a family. It is absolutely bonkers. These are things that cannot be put right later. If key moments in life pass you by, you will not get them back. We really need to wake up to this.

But as I settle back in Ireland, I am grateful that that we are among the lucky ones who are able to afford a home, and that we'll be able to raise our daughter well here, surrounded by a loving family, on both sides of the Atlantic now. I would hope to think that in my business so far, I've genuinely sought to create a positive impact in what we do. And if that is my approach in business, then logically it has to extend further. Now that I'm home, I feel really strongly that I'd like to try and make a difference with the problems that I see around me.

I am not sure yet how I can contribute publicly to life in Ireland, but it is not my personality to sit by and watch it get worse. The tough lessons I've learned in business and in life during my years in the US will stand to me as I go forward as a 35-year-old with a lot to say, a lot to do, and a lot to give back. I'll be focused on helping find solutions for those who feel unrepresented and unheard, similar to the ignored pain patients we are working for with Nutriband. The story is not over yet.

About the Author

Gareth Sheridan is an award winning entrepreneur, businessman and founder of Nutriband Inc., of which he is currently CEO. He received a B.Sc. in Business and Management from Dublin Institute of Technology in 2012 and in 2014 was Ireland's 'Young Entrepreneur of the Year'.

Gareth turned a business school thesis into a successsful enterprise while in his twenties, painting houses in Dublin to support himself. Then he brought it to the US, braving hard knocks along the way, navigating the shark-fest of public trading. In 2021, with the help of some great partners, his company was listed on the NASDAQ.

Today, his company Nutriband has its sights on Unicorn Status as it aims to become a billion dollar concern in the pharmaceutical industry, with breakthrough products in development, and trading established in 45 countries.

Gareth Sheridan returned to Ireland in 2025, where he now lives with his wife, Heidi and daughter Róe.

see more at: www.GarethSheridan.com

Tara
PRESS

www.ingramcontent.com/pod-product-compliance
Lightning Source LLC
Chambersburg PA
CBHW041209220326
41597CB00030BA/5152